W9-BGM-411

THE SIMPLE GUIDE TO
THE
ROMAN CATHOLIC
CHURCH

ABOUT THE AUTHOR

EDMUND HARTLEY was born in Kent, England, in 1932 into a Catholic family and has three brothers. Educated first by the Benedictines who asked him to leave, his schooling was completed by the Xaverian Brothers. Considered intellectually mediocre, he was put to Art School where he obtained the appropriate diplomas. National Service (1953-55) followed and ended with the award of a Commission. Then, at the age of 23, having decided that the Catholic priesthood was the highest possible human attainment, he was accepted for training and began his studies (1955-61) at St John's Seminary, near Guildford, Surrey, along with two of his brothers. A period as a curate followed, after which he was drafted into the Army again, this time as a Chaplain. As a priest in service uniform for over 18 years he spent time in Germany, Malaya, and the UK. Since leaving the Army in 1983, he has been looking after a parish in south-east Kent.

DRAWINGS BY IRENE SANDERSON

List of Illustrations

Ruins of the amphitheatre (Colosseum) in Rome	8
The Square outside St Peter's, Rome	16
Twelfth-century mosaic of St Peter	27
'Adoration of the Magi' – Domenico Ghirlandaio	38
'The Deposition' – Pietro Lorenzetti	57
Celebration of Holy Mass	85
Holy Shroud of Turin	100
Grotto of Massabielle, Lourdes	130

THE SIMPLE GUIDE TO

THE
ROMAN CATHOLIC
CHURCH

Edmund Hartley

GLOBAL BOOKS LTD

Public Library New London, CT

282
H

Simple Guides ● Series 3
WORLD RELIGIONS

The Simple Guide to
THE ROMAN CATHOLIC CHURCH
By Edmund Hartley

First published 1997 by
GLOBAL BOOKS LTD
PO Box 219, Folkestone, Kent, England CT20 3LZ

© Global Books Limited 1997

All rights reserved. No part of this publication
may be reproduced, stored in a retrieval system,
or transmitted in any form or by any means
without prior permission in writing
from the Publishers.

ISBN 1-86034-023-7

British Library Cataloguing in Publication Data
A CIP catalogue entry for this book
is available from the British Library

Distributed in the USA & Canada by
THE TALMAN CO. INC., New York

Set in Futura 10½ on 11½pt by Bookman, Slough
Printed in Great Britain by The Cromwell Press, Wiltshire

Contents

List of Illustrations   2
Foreword   9

1   **Origins**   12
    ☐ Past, Present & Future?   13
    ☐ Roots in Judaism   14
    ☐ Archaeology Can Be Helpful   17
    ☐ Greek Influence   18
    ☐ 'Fish' A Christian Symbol   18

2   **History**   19
    ☐ Paganism   20
    ☐ Life in Canaan   21
    ☐ A View of Uniqueness & Exclusivity   22
    ☐ Baptism: A Sign of Belonging   23
    ☐ 'Afterlife' & 'Reward'   24
    ☐ Inclusive not Exclusive   25
    ☐ Great Expectations   26
    ☐ 'A Man for All Seasons'   28
    ☐ The Needs of Our Age   29
    ☐ Roman Advance & Birth of Jesus Christ   31
    ☐ Jewish Self-image & History   32
    ☐ Who Recorded What?   32

3   **Founder**   34
    ☐ 'Completing' History   34
    ☐ The Gospels   36
    ☐ 'Good News'   36
    ☐ Founder? Leader? Starter?   37
    ☐ The Ten Commandments   40
    ☐ Completion & Fulfilment   41

4   **Aims & Christian Beliefs**   42
    ☐ Aims of Christianity   44
    ☐ How Christians Think of Themselves   44

5   **The Sin Thing**   46

	Primitive Notions of Good & Evil	47
	Evil 'The Absence of Good'	48
	General Notions of Sin	49
	The Psalmist & Sin	50
	'Time-conditioning'	51
	Early Christian View of Sin	52
	Penance, Punishment & Repentance	53
6	**Teachings & Doctrines [I]**	**56**
	Understanding Death	56
	What Can I Do for You?	59
	The Trinity	60
	The Apostle's Creed	63
7	**'Judgement' & 'Deliverance'**	**64**
	From Judgement to Forgiveness	65
	Relief When We Are 'Let Off'	66
	'Abuse' of Forgiveness?	67
	Restoration of Innocence	68
	Who Is to Judge?	69
8	**Myths**	**71**
	Definition of 'Myth'	72
9	**Faith & Morals**	**74**
	Aristotle's 'First Cause'	75
	The 'Faith Journey'	77
	Recognizing 'Truth'	78
	Morals	79
	God & the Neighbour	80
	The 'Morals' Debate	81
	What 'Rights?'	83
10	**Practices**	**84**
	Sacrifice	86
	The Eurcharist	87
	Resurrection	88
	Holy Mass	89
	The 'Sacrifice' of the Mass	90
	Sundays & Holy Days	90

☐ Other Feast Days   92
☐ Other Catholic Practices   93

11 Teachings & Doctrines [II]   95
☐ Responding to the Commandments   96
☐ The Iconoclasts & the Eucharist   98
☐ The Holy Shroud of Turin   101
☐ The 'Development' of Doctrine   102
☐ What the Early Christians Wanted to Know   103
☐ Dogmas   103
☐ The Truths of the Apostle's Creed   104
☐ Henry VIII 'Defender of the Faith'   105
☐ Errors & Heresies   105
☐ The Reformation   106
☐ Bible History   107
☐ What is Meant by 'Grace'   108

12 Priesthood & Laity   110
☐ Priestly Clothes   111
☐ The Monasteries & Education   112
☐ The Structure of the Catholic Church   113
☐ The Administration of the Catholic Church   114
☐ The Church Hierarchy   115

13 Liturgy & Sacred Texts   117
☐ 'Symbols' & 'Sight'   119
☐ The Seven Sacraments   122
☐ 'Christ's Role in the World'   124
☐ The Catholic Position on Life & Death   125
☐ Is There Another Name for God?   127

14 Pilgrimages & Holy Places   128
☐ Holy Places   128
☐ 'The Faith Journey' Revisited   132

Bibliography & Further Reading   133
Notes   134
List of Popes   137
Books of the Bible   140
Index   142

The ruins of the amphitheatre (the Colosseum) in Rome, built in AD80, famous for its shows of Christians being slaughtered by gladiators and wild beasts

Foreword

God as Creator & Designer of the Universe

THE PICTURE of His Holiness Pope John Paul II, on the front cover of this guide, gives the impression of his having all the troubles of the world on his shoulders. 'Better him than me', you might think. You would be right. As we shall see later there is a sense in which this is the responsibility that he has been chosen to bear. As one wag said: 'Responsibilities are to be shouldered, not carried under your arm!'

Over the centuries, and usually as the result of changes of an economic and often a political nature, popular systems of thought have taken root and effectively altered people's attitudes about many things. We modify the ways in which we communicate with one another; and as each change is later found to be wanting, there is a further development. It is these 'developments' that begin to be questioned, and, as invariably happens, each development is expected to justify itself.

In our own era, the Greeks reckoned themselves to be pioneers in the 'thinking process'. One might mention Thales, Anaximanda, Heraclitus, Plato, Aristotle etc., to set the scene. As far as they were concerned, they never felt the need to question their positions because they considered their systems to be self-evident! Indeed, much of their thinking continues to form the basis of life in the West. However, it is only when new and unforeseen problems arise, for which these 'systems' provide no answer, that new, or at least fresh, approaches are required.

When a system cannot answer certain questions then it has to be changed, or superseded. A brief glance at the political activity in twentieth-century Europe will make this clear. Sixteenth-century Europe, however, saw the emergence of the New Learning. As part of the Renaissance, a movement that had already begun earlier in the previous century, the justification for Christianity as a 'system' came in for serious questioning. Prior to this, anyone with the temerity to do so was severely dealt with; but popular opinion had grown to such a degree by this time that the Catholic Church could no longer be satisfied with 'sending a gun-boat' to deal with religious unrest.

'Onward Christian soldiers, marching as to war', a Methodist Christian hymn of the nineteenth century, admirably describes the Catholic Church's self-image during the late Middle Ages. Those trained in the

Greek system (then known as 'Scholastics') set themselves the task of laying out those 'thought principles' that supported Christian theological (doctrinal and moral) issues. Generally speaking, much of their material was partisan; to which modern-day atheists, like the successors of Bertrand Russell, took grave exception. 'How can you call a philosophy valid' he asked, 'when it argues to a conclusion already held to be absolute?' A very good question indeed – until you discover yet another principle, also held by the Scholastics, that 'philosophy is the *handmaid* of theology'.[1] Most people find this statement quite acceptable apart from those, of course, who deny the validity or even the existence of 'theology'!

Philosophy concerns what we know about 'thinking'; Theology concerns what we know about what 'God' has revealed. 'A healthy mind in a healthy body' is an old Latin principle that supports the idea that good medicine also enhances good thinking; like the axiom: 'Never send a soldier into battle on an empty stomach!'

What you are being offered here is not so much a support for Catholic thinking – since, generally speaking, Catholics probably do not think like this anyway! Nor is it offered as a defence or justification for Catholic principles. There is no pretence here, I hope, to be overtly philosophical or even theological. It is offered merely as (hopefully) one informative guide to the origins of Catholic Christianity and its practices as they are seen developing over the centuries.

Edmund Hartley

1 Origins

Basilica of the Holy Sepulchre, Jerusalem

'THE NORTH GATE'S on your left as you go out; so turn right, then take the first on the left and go down to the "T" junction and look for an opening on your right between the shops.' Totally enclosed by tall faded walls and a few steps down, a large courtyard emerged from out of the gloom. It was early morning. Looming across in the corner one could see two huge doorways under a Gothic arch. The one on the left was open; the other, closed up in the twelfth century, had not been opened since. At 5.30am all was dark inside save for three or four 40-watt light bulbs which hung down like glowing tassels. The only sound came from a dim corner where a monk with a white cloth cap on his dark head was chanting from a book on a desk. Oblivious to a stranger standing behind him in the darkness, he continued to read an old Coptic script by the light of the sputtering tallow candle he held in his hand. All around was dusty and unkempt. Behind him nondescript hangings curtained off a small apse which had been waiting – probably for months – to be refurbished.

At 6.00am an organ started up somewhere in the shadows and drowned the monk's dirge. This music accompanied a Latin rite procession which wandered away in the distance, to a remote altar. It felt like having stepped back in time. Here was altogether another world! Accustomed now to the gloom, I stood for an age where, for generations, other people have stood and wondered. This was a hallowed place which somehow cast its own particular spell. . . . a spell that dissolved an hour or two later as I stepped out into the sunlight of the courtyard of the Basilica of the Holy Sepulchre in the old city of Jerusalem.

Past, Present & Future?

The past, rather like the future, is in the dark; because it is not in the 'here and now'. The sun shining *today* is much more important than it shining *yesterday*. We can only see stars when it is dark – because they are so small they show up better. In fact, when looking at a star we are looking into the past – since the light we now see left that star a thousand years ago. To look into our past we need some light. But the light we need is often insufficient. Hindsight is described as 20/20 vision – 'the clearest way of seeing'. 'The further away from the game the more we can see of the play', when the overall picture becomes clearer. It is also said that 'distance lends enchantment to the view' – which is usually, but not always, true!

In moving great boulders for building purposes, Bronze Age people found that felled trees, when rolling side by side, proved a useful means of transport; however, one does not suppose for a moment that anyone *then* thought 'This is how they'll eventually discover the wheel!' It does seem, though, that the *more* we can see of the past, the greater the chance we have of understanding how and when things began. The *less* we know of the past, of course, the more difficult it is to answer certain queries – such as our present question: 'What were the Origins of Catholicism?' So we begin at the beginning, which is usually the best place to start. . . .

□

Roots in Judaism

The primitive herdsman's livelihood depends on his finding fresh grazing for his flock. He is dependent on knowing when and where it is going to rain next and, if he is down on his luck, he will look for someone to make it rain for him. Without understanding how the seasons work, our nomad will accept that, if he finds and make friends with the one who can make it rain, all will be well. . . . and if the 'rain-maker' happens to be a god, so be it – it will not be long before he is 'praying' or 'sacrificing something valuable' in order to get this god to do what he wants. All types of religious belief and practice begin like this, and, as far as we can see, the origins of Christianity are no different from the origins of any other cult.

Where there *is* a difference, it is that Christianity happens to be the development of a previous world religion which still exists: Judaism. One ought to say here that, to try to outline the origins of Christianity without already having looked at the origins of Judaism, would be like saying: because the sky is cloudy this morning, 'The sun is not shining!'

We cannot begin to understand Judaism without at the same time opening her Book. The Jewish Sacred Scriptures, known as the Holy Bible, proclaim the story of their 'Beginnings', honour their Patriarchs (Abraham, Isaac & Jacob) and give the gradual development of their history as a Nation. *Genesis* (the first word in the Greek translation of the Hebrew Bible) is the first book of the Bible and it is the only direct source we have for the history of these Patriarchs whose period is generally reckoned to be c2000-1700 BC – late Bronze Age[2].

It would be well to remember here that the Bible is the story of the beginning of things as seen by the Hebrew people. While it is probably the best known work of its kind, it is not the only one. The Semitic peoples, of which the Hebrews are one group, knew other traditions, some of which are no longer available to us – ancient sources – the existence of which can be traced in these Scriptures. What makes the 'history' in the Bible different from other 'histories' is that these writers disregarded anything that did not in some way relate to, or reflect upon, the development of their perceived relationship with their God. Such documented sources are to be found in museums, and so, although there is not much mention of them outside the Bible, the Patriarchs cannot just be the mythical characters that earlier scholarship thought them to be.

The Square outside St Peter's, Rome

Archaeology Can Be Helpful

Archaeological discoveries in the Near East have shown that the biblical descriptions of the Patriarchs and their era are remarkably accurate – far too accurate, in fact, to be thought of as inventions, or to be dismissed as having no historical foundation. Hindsight tells us that it would not have been possible for such episodes to have been composed in that part of the world, the near East, without some valid historical memory serving as a link with the past. We might begin to realize that these patriarchal traditions are not *just* or *merely* historical facts. They happen to belong to a type of literary genre that we would call 'family tradition'. This means that they will have received a certain amount of 'orientation' in the course of their transmission from one generation to the next, uniting, as they obviously would, various and indeed disparate elements in the process. This last consideration, however, does not prevent us from placing the Patriarchs in their correct historical perspective in the light of literary and archaeological data available today.

The Patriarchs are the first of a line of people, including kings, military leaders, priests, prophets, rebels, seers (each generation producing its own) who, over roughly the next 1700 years, look forward to an age of peace and prosperity. It will take another 1000 years for these people, beginning again with the Patriarchs, to find out, after all, that there is only one God – and, surprise – surprise, this God would be the God of the Hebrews. . . . and it would be *this* God who would somehow bring about this peace!

From about 1720BC, however, the Hebrews had about 400 years of a somewhat contrary experience, ending up as slaves, in Egypt. There they became familiar with the Egyptian religion with all its gods: Osiris, Isis with son Horus – the reigning Pharaoh sharing his divinity – with temples at Memphis and Karnak etc. Aristotle, much later (300BC) in Greece, was 90 before he came to realize that there could only be one God. A pagan, he had somehow managed to reason this out on his own without the benefit of such material as the Hebrew Scriptures.

Greek Influence

Greek thinking had a considerabe impact on the transmission of biblical material in the early years of Christianity. After all, the Greeks were the first to translate the Hebrew Biblical scrolls (round about 270BC), and their translation is known as the Septuagint.

'FISH' – A Christian Symbol

Greek for 'Fish': **I X Θ Υ Σ** (ιχθυζ) pronounced 'ikthus': (below in Roman script) stands for the following: I (*Iesus*) Ch (*Christ*) Th(eo) of *God* U *Son* S(ator) *Saviour*

2 History

Medieval monk with illuminated manuscript

THE CATHOLIC CHURCH is Christian and Christianity, like Judaism, of which it is the fulfilment, is an historical religion. It is possible to trace its roots back into the past, just as it is possible to trace any evolving phenomena. Latin and Greek commentators of that time have traced Jewish and Christian movements in the early years, and their writings often support records that we find in the Bible.

An 'historical religion' is described as one in which the God worshipped is a God who has revealed Himself to men *in* human history – a God who has done certain things that are facts of history – a God who has made known – 'revealed' – who He is, as well as what He wants in the matter of human moral conduct. Christianity, as a revealed religion, will tend to see 'morality' – or the 'rectitude of human behaviour' – as universal and unchanging. Herein lies our first difficulty since, no matter what we think it to be, 'Revelation' (the word we use to describe 'God-speaking-to-his-people') can only be perceived through human experience.

Every human experience brings with it elements of interpretation depending on the person who has the experience. One only has to compare evidence from all those bystanders who have witnessed the same event. Such evidence may then be coloured as the result of further experiences by the same witnesses. When finally committed to writing, the expression of that event could well appear to be very different from the initial experience of the event.

This why it takes so long for 'Revelation' to be understood as such. However, once it *has* been recognized for what it is, or, to put it another way, once there appears to be no other explanation for it, then there will come a time, one imagines, (seeing it to be 'God's Word') that it will become the foundation on which 'human morality' will be based. It will then gradually become a universal guide, and unchanging, no matter how often human *mores* may change. This is what differentiates Christianity, an 'historical' religion from paganism, which has always been its bed-fellow.

Paganism

Paganism is divorced from history in that it has no

gods that stand outside history, or that can intervene in history. Paganism normally finds its gods by personalizing, mythologizing, natural forces – hence 'myths' (p. 71). From pagan religions set in time, no timeless or unchanging morality can derive. In fact, pagan moralities, which have sometimes been of a very high order, have always been the possession of those few who have the mind and leisure to discover some permanent values in the world about them *without* having recourse to their gods.

It was into such a pagan culture that the Israelite Hebrews settled, having returned from Egypt in the fourteenth century BC. With their God of Promise and Command, they came into a land which was already the home of such gods as Baal and Ashera, Anath and Kadesh, deities in whose service every conceivable lust and vice had been practised and sanctified. Magic, superstition, ritual debauchery and prostitution, human sacrifice, living children burnt as offerings to a god called 'The King'; while the aged and the handicapped were killed and buried beneath their thresholds to ward off demons.

Life in Canaan

Such was the folklore of Canaan, the Israelites' new home. Here, as they had in Egypt, they familiarized themselves with the values of an already settled people. It was also far easier, though, and much more pleasant, to learn the unsettling vices of the Canaanites. The Israelites had little knowledge of arts and crafts, of agriculture, and proprietorship. They now found models and teachers ready to hand, but they also felt the tug of Canaan in other and more devious directions as well.

As the indigenous folk had so much to offer, Canaan being a 'Land flowing with milk and honey', the Israelites, with their primitive mind-set, saw that this could only be because the Canaanite gods had made it so lush and prosperous. This was the argument of the day, and it was a powerful one. What may be shocking, yet thoroughly understandable, is to learn is that they even used the names of pagan deities for their God of Promise! Each successive Hebrew generation, however, produced its own Prophets who inveighed against the dangers of falling in with such pagan practices. It was the Prophets who laid the subsequent misfortunes of their people at the feet of all who, forgetting their God-given Promises, had succumbed to this pagan influence.

□

A View of Uniqueness & Exclusivity

From its beginnings Christianity will appear to have been 'exclusive'. In so far as it is a development of Judaism, which had its own initiation rites, this would be true. But there is also the element of the 'unique' about Christianity that we might consider now.

To some extent, all historical religions are exclusive in their notions of the origins of the world and its peoples. Christianity, like Judaism, is just as exclusive and for the same reasons. Its members see themselves as belonging to a 'club' and, having been through all their particular initiation procedures, understandably consider themselves 'set apart' from those who have not. For the Jews this exclusiveness is received at birth, from a Jewish mother, ratified initially by Circumcision (a Bronze Age custom of indeterminate origin) and later also by 'knowledge of the Mosaic

Law'; and by a more recent custom to mark a boy's 'coming of age' at 13 – 'Bar Mitzvah'. [The Mosaic Law is found in the *Book of Deuteronomy* – one of the first five Books of the Old Testament of the Bible or, to give it its Jewish name, *Torah*]

This Jewish exclusiveness can be recognized in its dealings with other tribal races. The Hebrews came to see themselves as a 'holy nation', sacred and dedicated to Yahweh (a Hebrew sacred name for God). Jews are still 'God's Chosen People'. The Christian development of this notion can be seen in that, more than just being members of a chosen race, Christians see themselves as members of a Family, with 'God' as its Father. It is with this notion that Christianity begins to develop away from Judaism – a development that is charted in the New Testament of the Bible.

Baptism: A Sign of Belonging

Christian exclusiveness is received in an initiation rite, which at the start was called by its Greek name, 'Baptism'. ['Christening', the English word for this ceremony, clearly has more meaning for us nowadays, but it did not come into common English usage until the Middle Ages.]

When people with a common interest consider the future in terms of organizing themselves to increase their numbers or to plan an enterprise, the normal procedure is to arrange a 'membership' where each agrees to a set of rules or a constitution. A card is received that marks his or her commitment to the newly constituted group. Whether or not the practice of Circumcision was imposed on the Hebrews by their God, or taken from a pagan observance with God's blessing, nonetheless, it was employed as a sign that distinguished the believer from those who were not circumcised. . .a simple initiation rite the *religious* significance of which surfaced rather later in about the sixth century BC.

In our own time Christians employ Baptism as a sign of belonging to the Christian community. During this ceremony certain vows are taken to demonstrate that this is not some idle performance but the marking of a person in such a way as to lead on to an adult commitment that will last through life.

'Afterlife' and 'Reward'

The assumption most people make is that Christianity, like every other tradition, including Judaism, is about what its members do for one another, or perhaps, more fundamentally, that it concerns what each must do 'to ensure good things in this life in order to get a good place in the hereafter!' Later, it will involve 'How I ought to behave to my Neighbour', but first and foremost it will be about 'No.1.' – 'Me'. Since no matter what particular view of life one holds to be 'politically correct' – what cannot be denied, in all honesty, is that: 'In my world, I come *first*, and after Me, my parents, my family, my friends, acquaintances etc., including my Neighbour'. 'I can't help but see that everything relates, in some way, to Me.'

Irritating though this statement may be, it will have to be admitted sooner or later that no one is born an altruist! Altruism has to be learnt – hence the Hebrew Commandment: 'As you love Yourself so must you love your Neighbour' – a maxim that is to be found in many other Codes of Conduct. At all events, it will be clear that *if* there is some sort of existence 'after death' then 'it will be solely my fault if I fail to get the best available' – a view supported by the Greek philosophers when talking about responsibility.

Inclusive not Exclusive

Christianity, like its predecessor Judaism and its successor Islam, has been 'Exclusive' since the beginning of its recorded history, even though this was not in the mind of its 'Founder'. For the Christian, anyone who does not believe in this one God is a pagan. [Islam tends to view non-Muslims as 'infidels', though this is not the teaching of the *Qur'ān*.] Christianity, however, does recognize its debt to Judaism by claiming a special relationship with the Hebrew God; but it adds that the fulfilment of this relationship seems to have been overlooked by Judaism.

Islam recognizes 'The Decalogue' (p. 40) and sees the Christ as a prophet. However, the Qur'ān does not quote from the Bible nor does it show that Muhammad had any personal contact with either the Jewish Scriptures or Christianity, though he certainly knew of Jews and Christians and perhaps knew something of their background.

It is not surprising that Christianity began with an opening of the doors not only to Jews who came to believe in Jesus Christ but also to 'all comers', slaves and citizens whether of high or low degree. After all, the disciples had been instructed by the Christ to preach the 'good news' to All Nations. However, to the early Church, it was paramount to protect this new Knowledge. With the removal of the pressure exerted on the Hebrews by the Law (p. 39), came the burgeoning of fresh ideas and, as Christianity spread, it was seen to be equally paramount that none of these be allowed to damage the Faith which had been described by the Christ, who had bequeathed it to them, as 'the pearl of great price' .

Soon, the 'building of structures', always necessary when it comes to managing an organization, was also seen by some of its leaders (those who began to take over from the Apostles) to be 'Christ given' and divinely inspired. This could not help but lead to a protectionism that would brook no threat to what was, as yet, not firmly established.

Hindsight again helps us to understand the human and helplessly secular mind-set of those who, once in possession of such a prize, would see in these ideas and divisions of opinion, as well as the denial of some of its tenets, threats to the Christian fulfilment of Christ's command to teach All Nations. Had they forgotten that the Christ would be with them to the end of time? (*Matthew* 28:20) or that Paul had told them that *nothing* could come between them and the love of God revealed to them in Christ Jesus?

Great Expectations

What does the world expect of the Church? Should it not stand for what is right in the face of opposition or should it give in to what is fashionably acceptable? (see the debate p. 81). The Middle Ages saw the continuing Christian harassment of Jews and Muslims and the ruthless way in which those found guilty of heresy were treated (p. 106). In Europe the Spanish Inquisition is an example of this. A little later, in England, we find the persecution of Catholics in Tudor times, beginning with the Dissolution of the Monasteries. Later, the fires of Smithfield marked a

Twelfth-century mosaic depicting St Peter in Roman dress (left) and Pope Cornelius (AD 251-3)

persecution of Protestants by Catholics; then the slaughter of the Anabaptists under Luther in Germany; then the forcible removal in the seventeenth and eighteenth centuries of 90% of the land in Ireland from its Catholic landlords; then the secularization of Catholic Church lands in nineteenth-century Germany.

Had Catholicism somehow become a threat to the new ideas which were growing with the Renaissance? Mankind seems doomed to be incapable of realizing its spiritual inheritance – could it be because of Man's sinfulness?

We have seen, however, a remarkable change recently in religious attitudes. The so-called 'Ecumenical Movement' of the twentieth century which seems to have developed as result of the reign of Pope John XXIII (p. 139) and the Second Vatican Council (1963-65) in Rome.

A Man for All Seasons

In his Play *A Man for All Seasons*, the author, Robert Bolt, has a court scene where Thomas More is asked to justify his 'conscience' in the matter of his unwillingness to sign to the Act of Supremacy (1535) whereby King Henry VIII makes himself 'Head of the Church in England'. More's life or death depends on his answer. Each party in this debate considers himself to be in the right and they reach an impasse. The Duke of Norfolk says: 'But damn it, Thomas, look at these names (those who had signed). You know these men! Can't you do what I did and come with us, for fellowship?'. Thomas replies gently: 'And when we stand before God and you are sent to Paradise for doing your 'conscience' and I am sent to Hell for not doing mine, will you come with me – for fellowship?'

The Needs of Our Age

We could close this section by remembering that all living persons are not only human beings, but persons, free to make up their minds about a lot of things, who are yet inescapably conditioned by tradition and prevailing opinions. 'It is essential (therefore) that the doctrine of the Church, certain and immutable,[3] to which we owe dutiful acceptance, be studied and explained in accordance with the needs of our own age. The Deposit of Faith is one thing; the manner in which it is presented is another.' (Part of Pope John XXIII's opening address at the Second Vatican Council.)

The Catholic Church provides the world with the teachings of Christ who authorized her existence in this changing world. This means that, teaching with Christ's authority which remains supreme, the Catholic Church must in someway share this supremacy.

The Promise

All religions that recognize an 'afterlife' will make much of a standard of life here, a particular quality of life in this world, so as to ensure a good place in whatever realm exists beyond the grave. Thus, great emphasis gets placed on living a good life now 'so as to reap an eternal reward'. However, apart from the initiation rites, the uniqueness of Christianity lies in the fact that *it is not just* what we do here that assures us of this 'eternal reward'. This uniqueness lies in the Promise God freely made to Abraham and his descendants. It has been described as a 'Covenant', and the terms of that Covenant stated that Abraham would become the Father of a great Nation. In the first statement of this Promise (*Genesis*: Chapter 12) no condition is mentioned! As far as we can tell, Abraham had been chosen to receive this Promise for no apparent reason. Like other great religious leaders of the past, none seems to have had any pedigree. They all appear from nowhere and then disappear afterwards. [When we come to its 'Founder' we will find yet another reason why Christianity would be called 'unique'.]

A promise had been made to Abraham by God and, though the Scriptures point to the innumerable mistakes and often the deliberate rejections of sound advice given by the Prophets, this same Promise was to be repeated again and again. As time goes by (and of course with hindsight operating again), we begin to see that, not only can nothing prevent this Promise being fulfilled, but it also appears, in the beginning, to have been made unconditionally!

It might be obvious that all history, whether written down or transmitted by word of mouth, depends almost totally on those responsible for its eventual composition. To have external sources that supply corroborating evidence is considered to be good fortune. Notwithstanding the existence of such sources, most people will be aware of the difficulties in constructing, for example, modern European history, since its authors emphasize certain events at the expense of others in order to support a prevailing point of view – be it political or economic. By and large, this partial attitude to the past affects all those engaged in transmitting events which lead to given conclusions that require their support. One has then to agree that even hindsight has its own drawbacks!

When Alexander the Great, the famous Greek general, defeated the Persians at the Granicus River (334BC) he took possession of Asia Minor. With access to Syria he then annexed the Eastern Mediterranean, establishing Alexandria, where Greek Jews would shortly be wanting their Sacred Books translated from the Hebrew. Greek fashions and ways also began to affect Jerusalem and pose a threat to the traditional Jewish way of life.

Roman Advance & Birth of Jesus Christ

Our history here is particularly concerned with the two kingdoms that were rivals for the control of Palestine. From the fourth century BC it had fallen under the protection of Alexander's successors: the Egyptian 'Ptolomies' and the Syrian 'Seleucids'. With the Greek ascendancy, even though Judea proper remained a relatively small self-contained area, having only loose contact with the rest of Palestine, everywhere began to experience the process of hellenization (the imposition of Greek culture and value systems).

The Jews were naturally restive as a result and there was some revolt against the Greeks who had been 'hellenizing' their neighbours for 170 years. The Roman Empire, however, now growing for some 750 years, had, by 63BC, incorporated the whole of that area into its Syrian Province, then ruled by a Roman legate, and for a time there was peace.

In 37BC the Emperor Octavian appointed Herod the Great as king. Herod died in about 8BC and about four years later Jesus Christ was born (around 4BC). He was born into a period of great turmoil and, among Jews, great expectations – of the coming of a Messiah who would bring to an end the Roman occupation of their country and an end to all foreign influence.

Jewish Self-image & History

Because of the Jewish national self-image, those parts of the Old Testament that appear to convey an on-going historical narrative use historical events to point out the overriding role of 'God-leading-his-people-from-slavery-to-freedom'. For instance, the defeat of this Nation in 721BC and again in 583BC as the result of their kings involving themselves in injudicious political manoeuvering is seen by biblical writers[4] as 'God punishing his people for their being unfaithful to his Law' (p. 39).

While these writers drew some questionable conclusions from the events they had recounted, there can be no doubt about the historical nature of the events themselves. If we have difficulty today in constructing the path of modern European history, it is not altogether a simple matter to disentangle historical material dating from the Near East as it was over 2,000 years ago. As a scientist perhaps sees history in terms of the evolution of man's efforts to harness the forces of nature, where every generation produces its new discoveries of things that were always there, the philosopher perhaps sees history in terms of the evolution of man's attempts to understand these forces and the underlying purposes behind them.

Who Recorded What?

By way of a detour, were one examining these ancient writers for some pedigree, we find, for instance, Tacitus (†c120AD), a classical Latin author, referring to Christianity as a 'foreign superstition' and he finds Nero '*setting-up*' the Christians for the Fire of Rome in 64AD for which they were all duly punished! Tacitus also mentions 'Christ' as the one from whom this name is derived. Suetonius (†c160) speaks of 'Chrestos' as the 'instigator of Jewish disturbances'. Pliny the Younger (†c113) a magistrate, speaks of Christianity as a 'depraved and extravagant superstition'. Trajan (†c117), Justin (†c150) and Tertullian (†240), among the better known writers of the second and third centuries looked on Christians as 'atheists'.

For 250 years Christians throughout the empire were persecuted with varying degrees of cruelty, with a brief respite under the Emperor Gallienus (261). Incidentally, the first time we come across the word 'catholic' is in a rescript of Constantine to Anulius, Proconsul of Africa in 313, and quoted by Eusebius, which contains an order for the restitution of confiscated Christian church property. It is amusing to note that while in Greek, 'catholic' means 'universal', in Latin it means 'finance controller'. Anyway, the Emperor Constantine discontinued the persecution of Christians and made Christianity the state religion; at which time the building of purposeful churches began which everyone agreed was a very good idea.

3 Founder

The Harrowing of Hell by Jesus Christ

'Completing' History

THERE IS NO ATTEMPT to describe 'Faith' in this guide, nor explain how it is that 'believing' is a technical expression for a special way of 'knowing someone'. The aim here is simply to lay out certain aspects of Catholicism that might be of interest to the casual reader.

Modern history declares Jesus Christ, born a Palestinian Jew, as the one from whom Christianity gets its name. His story is to found in the New Testament section of the Bible. However, hindsight again would tell us that his story begins rather earlier – to be precise, with the *Book of Genesis* with which the Bible begins.

An understanding of the place of Jesus Christ in the development of Western civilization would require some knowledge of both sections of the Bible since he is seen by many to complete that history. It is common knowledge among Christians that the 'New' Testament somehow completes the 'Old' Testament.

The story of Christ is peculiar, however, in that it appears to have been written back to front! (Perhaps Agatha Christie's novels are composed the same way – starting with the conclusion so as to know how she wants the story to end; and then working back to the beginning.) Had Christ *not* been seen and recognized within days after his death, his memory may well have sunk without trace, and posterity would remember nothing of him. But, by those who remembered him during his life-time, he is described as having had an amazing grasp of man's condition without appearing to have had much education. He is reported to have said extraordinary things despite the fact that he had none of the qualifications, for instance, of a person like Sirach, who wrote the *Book of Ecclesiasticus.*

Jesus Christ is reported to have done some extraordinary things – quite beyond the ability of Elisha, a Jewish miracle worker of the ninth century BC (*2Kings2*). Even so, there might not have been much to write about had there been any doubt at the time that **Jesus Christ had risen from the dead** – a fact which, for centuries, has been questioned, debated and even denied. But, however unlikely that event may appear, it has not prevented subsequent generations from accepting it. Those first to be aware of the events which led to his death had to tell everyone they met how it came about and then go on to show how these events demonstrated that this *had* to be the Person expected by the Patriarchs and also by all the Prophets of the Old Testament.

The Gospels

The four main traditions that were soon to grow from this small beginning are now known as 'Gospels'. Gospels are recognized as writings which accord to traditions associated with the Disciples 'Matthew', 'Mark', 'Luke' and 'John' (Anglicized forms of their original Aramaic and Greek names). What we do know from these short works and those of some of his other Disciples, is that the ideas they then had of Christ could only have been expressed in the language which was familiar to them and their readers – and that was the language of the Old Testament! It took time before the meaning of this 'extraordinary phenomenon' began to dawn on the people who first listened to Christ's Disciples.

'Good News'

Following Old Testament analysis, those responsible for the Gospel (an early Christian word meaning 'good news') – saw the Christ as 'someone like Moses' (c1400BC)[5] who had actually seen and spoken with God, or 'Elijah-returned-to-life' (a prophet of the ninth century BC), or 'Jeremiah' (a prophet of the seventh century BC). Some even thought him to be a reincarnation of John the Baptist who had recently been beheaded! The Gospel writers, and those who assisted them, were not the first nor the only ones to be lost for words to express adequately what they had now come to realize.

Founder?/Leader?/Starter?

'Founder' is the word we use for someone who starts an organization ordered to the benefit of others – be it a Bank, Hospital, Parish/Benefice, Political/Economic Society, College/School etc. But we have no word that is appropriate for the person who 'started' Christianity because, as a movement, it did not, so to speak, 'start from scratch'! As far as we can tell, Christianity has been in the process of developing since the beginning of Hebrew-recorded history.

Even with some misgivings, most people would now recognize the validity of Darwin's Theory of Evolution. An examination of their antecedents demonstrates an evolutionary process that has brought about significant changes in the semblance and behaviour of animals. In the same way, one traces the development – evolution – of Ideas down the centuries and comes to understand why it is that some people think in this way and others think in that way. The principles involved in Darwin's *Origin of Species* can also be employed in discussing such movements, the survival of which are as much dependent on fashion as his 'Species' are on natural selection and both depend on the survival of the 'fittest'!

Might we not consider Christianity as such a movement? It is highly improbable that Jesus Christ would have replaced a movement (Judaism) which was already a 'going concern'. To have tried to do so would have been disproportionate anyway and unlikely to succeed. He merely reminded his contemporaries, in the same way as the Prophets had done before him, that, just as their listeners had misunderstood the meaning of the message of the Old

Domenico Ghirlandaio (1449-94) 'The Adoration
of the Magi', Florence

Testament, they, too, would fail to understand who *he* was and what *he* was doing. But the nub of his problem was how to convince, especially the religious folk (you know, the ones who always 'think they're right'), not that they were wrong (that would be counter-productive) but that there was something the matter with their attitude regarding what they *thought* was true and incontrovertible. And this problem lingers still.

In the first century of the Christian era, the popular idea among some of its preachers was that Christ *had* produced something new – which had really *replaced* the Jewish tradition with all its rules and regulations (all somehow related to the 'Ten Commandments', also known as the 'Decalogue'). Others accepted that Christianity was merely an 'update' on Judaism and that Jewish orthodoxy would eventually welcome the development. Both were right in their own way and felt there was nothing to lose in discussing it.

Though the rules of the Decalogue are chiefly in the negative, it is from this simple list that a set of over 600 supplementary rules gradually developed. To break any one of them was considered 'sinful'. By the time the Decalogue was committed to writing (in the tenth century BC) it was then recognized as God's Law and thus the fact that the Mesopotamian Code of Hammurabi (p. 80) had provided the main source for it, had been discarded.

Many Christians felt that Christ, a Jew himself, was merely *uplifting* traditions with which everyone was familiar and naturally they considered it quite reprehensible for Jews not to recognize this transformation, especially as it was so clearly to their advantage. In fact, to such an extent did the Jewish

The Ten Commandments

The Decalogue (*Exodus* 20: 3-17 & 20)[6] was given to the frightened people in order 'to keep them from sinning':-

1. You shall have no gods except me. You shall not make yourself a carved image or any likeness of anything in heaven or on the earth beneath or in the waters under the earth; you shall not bow down to them or serve them. For I, Yahweh your God, am a jealous God and I punish the father's fault in the sons, the grandsons, and the great-grandsons of those who hate me; but I show kindness to thousands of those who love me and keep my commandments.

2. You shall not utter the name of Yahweh your God to misuse it, for Yahweh will not leave unpunished the man who utters his name to misuse it.

3. Remember the Sabbath day and keep it holy. For six days you shall labour and do all your work, but the seventh day is a Sabbath for Yahweh your God. You shall do no work that day, neither you nor your son nor your daughter nor your servants, men or women, nor your animals nor the stranger who lives with you. For in six days Yahweh made the heavens and the earth and the sea and all that these hold, but on the seventh day he rested; that is why Yahweh has blessed the Sabbath day and made it sacred.

4. Honour your father and your mother so that you may have a long life in the land that Yahweh your God has given to you.

5. You shall not kill.

6. You shall not commit adultery.

7. You shall not steal.

8. You shall not bear false witness against your neighbour.

9. You shall not covet your neighbour's house.

10. You shall not covet your neighbour's wife, or his servant, man or woman, or his ox, or his donkey, or anything that is his.

majority protest at this 'new-fangled' treatment of the 'divine inheritance' they held so dear, that by the turn of the first century Jewry had expelled from its synagogues all those Jews who had turned to Christianity.

In an almost tit-for-tat exercise Christians turfed out all Jews who would not make up their minds about Christ being the Messiah. One might also say that the European phenomenon known as The Reformation which 'happened' in the sixteenth century, was almost a mirror image of what has just been described. Certainly Protestantism could only be described in the terms of that to which it gave rise and use this word 'protest' – but that interesting development is treated elsewhere (see *The Simple Guide to the Protestant Tradition*)

Completion and Fulfilment

While there is a conflict of opinion, here the Christian position is that, rather than 'founding' this movement, Christ, as he is seen in the New Testament, really fulfils the aspirations of the people of the Old Testament. Further than this though, subsequent developments seem to show that as the New completes the Old Testament, Christians by and large now hold that Jesus Christ completes, and gives meaning to, the whole History of Mankind. So though we are restricted to the word 'Founder', it does not really express what hindsight has told us of the matter. No doubt you will agree that 'Completer' or 'Fulfiller' or even 'Facilitator' all sound terrible!

4 Aims & Christian Beliefs

Baptism of Christ

A GLASS OF WATER is either half full or half empty depending on how you see it. An optimist has a generous view of things. The pessimist is always slightly envious of this but will still say that, on incontrovertible evidence, the 'way of things' is always downwards. Even with his depressing view, the pessimist will still try to make things better for himself.

The poor, 'who are always with us' may look with envy on those who are rich, but the tycoon, looking down from his office, will envy the paper-boy he sees whistling his merry way from one delivery to the next. It is true that Christianity initially provides the poor with something to which they can look forward – just as the Old Testament looks forward, with some certainty, to its fulfilment. Superficially, Christianity discovers to everyone who looks at it a means of recognizing his or her worth as a person. Superficially, it teaches equality and indeed preaches 'human rights'; and while it gives the optimist a reason for optimism, to the pessimist it does give an excuse, if not a reason, for being happy. The Aims of Christianity, however, are more profound than the mere expression of 'Goodness' and 'Well-being' and how these necessities are to be achieved.

Christians hold that Jesus Christ completes the History of Mankind. Without his presence the purpose for everything disintegrates and nothing makes much real sense. The reason why this extraordinary statement should be made here is that Jesus Christ is 'God-made-Man'. Man's world is inseparably part of God's immense Universe. While this 'fact' is now held to be incontrovertible it is difficult to demonstrate such a fact just from what Christ's friends thought of him and from their references to him in the New Testament. Schooled as they all were in Old Testament thought and language, it would have been impossible for his Disciples to have acclaimed Christ to be 'God-made-Man', especially seeing that they thought of him as a 'reincarnation' of one of the Prophets![7]

The Hebrews, as far as we know, were the first Unitarians. 'Hear O Israel; the Lord your God is one God'. [Islam is also Unitarian: 'We have only one God, Allah; and Mohammed is his prophet]. It is one thing for someone to proclaim Jesus Christ as the

'Holy-One-of-God', or 'Messiah', 'Son of David' – but for anyone of his time to have said: 'Christ is God Himself' – emphatically No! That would have been a blasphemy! During the early centuries of the Church, Christians were so scared of blasphemy that some continued to deny it. Many people still do today.

Aims of Christianity

The Aims of Christianity are:-
● To encompass the world with the knowledge that all persons are made in God's Image;
● That all persons are adopted as God's Children and able to address Him as 'Father';
● That because they are seen now to share, in some way, his Godly nature, they are therefore destined, all sins having been forgiven, to inherit, in some way, God's Eternal Life.

This is what is meant by the **Good News**, and Jesus Christ authorized his friends to preach it to the whole world beginning from Jerusalem. It would take another 325 years for a codified set of Christian truths to begin to be presented to the world.

How Christians Think of Themselves

While living in the present, some races of people pride themselves on their past history. Others consider their past of little consequence compared with their present interests, and others, depending on their conditions, look solely to the future. These trends are easily recognized in the way Catholics think of themselves. All religions, pagan or otherwise, have notable similarities and Christianity admits to having taken material from pagan cults for its own purposes. What further distinguishes Christianity from other world religions is not so much what it teaches, but the emphasis it places on what their God has done to them and what He continues to do for them, rather than what they are expected to do for Him.

And yet Christianity continues to tell people what 'each must do to inherit eternal life'. We are limited by time and place in this world which is one reason that we still seem to be 'restricted' to continue to live here with the conditioning of the past, which we cannot escape. No matter how liberated we might think we are today, rather than 'living in the presence of Christ', Christians still seem to 'live in Old Testament times' where obedience to the Law is reckoned to be the condition of reaching their eternal destiny. We are now God's children:[8] is it not strange that the meaning of this simple statement is still beyond us? What more do we need to know?

Good Question!

5 The Sin Thing

SIN IS A WORD that has already been mentioned. Although it is an uncomfortable word, it serves to introduce a question which has bothered us for centuries. With talk about quality of life, a good place, living a good life, and now 'our obedience to the Law' being the 'condition of our reaching our eternal destiny', sooner or later we will have to deal with that which appears to militate against the success of our efforts to achieve this: namely the *Problem of Evil*.

With or without an interest in religion, the problem of *right and wrong*, and how to deal with this question has bothered all who pride themselves on being able to tell the difference. Culture and tradition appear to dictate which is which. We find occasionally that what is deemed 'good' in some (e.g., the extermination of enemies) is found to be 'evil' in others. Again, as the possession of what is thought good leads to happiness (something that everyone seems to want above all else) then the dispossession of what is thought to be good leads to unhappiness.

In an effort to understand this problem many cultures have developed the idea that, since individual people, as well as communities, were often at loggerheads with one another, there must be separate principles of Good and of Evil that are somehow responsible for this state of affairs. The solution was to personify both of them, and watch the continual conflict between them hoping that, eventually, the Good would triumph over the Evil. This appears to have been the mind-set of those who, in the tenth century BC, began to gather their material with a view to composing a 'history of God's Chosen People'. The way in which we are told the conquering Hebrews carried out their invasion of what is now called the West Bank of the Jordan will leave us in no doubt about what *they* thought was right and wrong. It is worth noting, however, that, according to the writers of the *Book of Joshua*, they had been told to exterminate the local population by no less a person than their God!

Primitive Notions of Good & Evil

The idea that there are two such principles (Good and Evil) always at war with one another is a primitive and a 'mythical' one. However, that notion is by no means the end of the matter and we will need to have another look at it later. The Old Testament view of Sin was a negative one in that it showed up the *inability* of the Hebrew people to observe the Law given them in the Ten Commandments and all disasters were seen, by most Old Testament writers, as 'punishments' for this.

It will not be recognized until well into the Christian era that although Good is in no way diminished or affected by the presence of Evil, Evil cannot abide the presence of Good. Truth, for instance, can cope with deliberate misunderstanding and even lies, but Falsehood collapses when faced with the Truth.

Evil – 'the Absence of Good'

Perhaps it would be nearer the mark to suggest that far from Good and Evil being two positive principles of equal but opposite power, it would be more accurate to speak of Evil as 'the absence of Good', rather like Coldness as the absence of Heat. We still see Sin in Old Testament terms: namely as a failure, frequently deliberate, to keep to the rules which were given, in the first place, to Man for the common good; and since the Ten Commandments comprised the Law given by God, not only will it be an offence against my Neighbour; Sin will be principally an offence against God.

☐

Catholics have always accepted the *Book of Genesis* as the account of the beginnings of Creation, and therefore felt, until recently, that Darwin's *Origin of Species*, in much the same way as, in 1633, Galileo's thesis,[9] was a threat to Church tradition. However, the 20th Ecumenical Council: 'Vatican I' (Rome 1869-

70), reminding us that philosophy is the *handmaid* of theology, states that not only does human reasoning brighten up supernatural Truth (which has been revealed by God), but that there can be no opposition between this reasoning and Faith. Since Reason cannot, therefore, be in opposition to Faith, it still appears to be somewhat disproportionate, to our way of thinking, that *Genesis* should propose that the Creator first places Man in a Paradise setting, and then places on him a condition on which his continuing status there depends. *Genesis* provides us with the Hebrews' setting for the way in which Sin enters Man's arena, and it is a setting that is accepted by all those contributors to the Bible who refer to it.

General Notions of Sin

However, it takes time for such as the findings of the First Vatican Council, to get through to the person in the street – even the Roman streets – for it was only recently, in 1992, that the Vatican decided to exonerate Galileo and say he was right after all.

There can be no denial that the Hebrew Scriptures constitute the historical Word of God dating as they do, initially, from 1000BC, and you may remember the remark (p. 32) that though 'those writers drew some questionable conclusions from the events they recounted, there could be no doubt about the historical nature of the events themselves'.

There can be no doubt now about the existence of Sin – there appears to have been rather a lot of it about, and for a very long time, and everyone knows about it. But how it came to be in the first place remains a problem. The Hebrew notion of Sin was a breaking of the Law. The *Book of Exodus* contains the official promulgation of the Law. . .so how could Sin be around before there was any Law to break?. This is one of the times when we realize that the story of Adam and Eve was composed after the Hebrews had learnt that Sin was about 'breaking God's Law'.

This question was first asked by Paul (*Romans* 5:13) The Scriptures tell us that *sin entered the world through one man*,[10] a statement based on the unquestioned notion that *Genesis* held the sole explanation for the beginning of everything. We also know that Christ is *the Lamb of God that takes away the sin of the world*[11] which, like Paul's remark, reflects a development that clearly goes beyond the thinking of the Old Testament.

While the Bible tells us that Sin is now simply effected by breaking God's Laws, apart from the *Genesis* account, we cannot demonstrate *how* Sin came into this world in the beginning or *how* it continues to be present. It does have something to do with Man's 'personal human nature' and is as Mysterious as is the Mystery of God's Forgiveness (p. 66) and as such the Church tells us that the existence of Sin is a matter of Faith.

In this discussion it is difficult not to find oneself 'out of one's depth' as it contains so many imponderables. This is why we can rightly call it a Mystery. The Church has bound itself inseparably to the Bible, not only because it constitutes the Word of God, but because it also serves as a link with our beginnings as Christians, and, to go back even further, with Man's beginnings as a Person.

The Psalmist and Sin

One aspect of Catholic teaching regarding Sin is its

relation to Death. The Hebrew Psalmist seeks the death penalty for sinners, and prays that God will punish, in this way, all His enemies (i.e. all who disobey Him). Naturally enough, such an attitude, as we have seen already, would be carried over into Christian thinking when Death begins to be seen as *the* punishment for Sin. . . . the idea that all men die because all men are sinners.[12]

In much the same way that the Hebrews inherited the Egyptian materialistic notion of the 'after-life' and reflected it even in the writing of the New Testament, so we find it supporting the Christian notion that 'a good life in this world will be rewarded hereafter with endless bliss; while an evil lifestyle here will deserve endless punishment'. Some Catholics still think in this way and speak of 'eternity' in terms of it being 'a very, very long time' or 'a time without end'. The use of the expression 'endless ages' to describe 'eternity' demonstrates our abysmal lack of an adequate language when we try to speak of a state where there is no time; but it does give us a marvellous example of 'time-conditioning'.

'Time-conditioning'

'Time-conditioning' is an expression which describes what happens when 'the language, which was used in the past to describe certain ideas, is gradually found to be inadequate; when those ideas have developed beyond the language that was used earlier to describe them'. [You find this examined when you are confronted with the notion of 'myth', p. 71.] Though we have developed some under-standing of the meaning of the word 'eternity', we can begin to tell you *what it is not* – but we still cannot tell you what it *is*!

The importance of this little detour will be recognized once you learn that Catholics tend to think that 'to die in a state of serious sin deserves eternal punishment'! For many Catholics this terrifying prospect would be sufficient to prevent them from remaining, for any length of time, in a state of being guilty of having seriously broken God's Law. This notion has been lifted piecemeal from pre-Christian ideas and has survived throughout the Church's history. While it is true to suggest that it would be seriously unworthy for 'a member of God's family deliberately to remain in such a state of guilt' it would be equally unworthy to deny that 'the Christ takes away the sins of the world'.

Early Christian View of Sin

The references in the New Testament to Sin and its Punishments concern chiefly the difficulties, experienced by the early Christians, of coming to terms with the death of Christ, and following those Apostolic missionaries who taught them that the Christ had *conquered and put an end to death*. . . Christians were encouraged to persevere in their new way of life in the face of great odds. It was also considered thoroughly reprehensible for anyone of them to sin by 'giving up'.

Dare one suggest, with others who have thought the same, that Sin exists so that God can show us His Love and Mercy? Is it possible that He would humiliate Himself to that degree. . . for Christ to put Himself into our hands and be at our disposal; or to put us in such a commanding position as held by Pontius Pilate when he sat in the Judgement seat on the first Good Friday to sentence Him to death? Dare one ask: How can the evil of Sin be part of God's plan?

However long we might like to speculate over all this there can be no doubt that we are stuck with the problem. Having recognized this over the centuries, Catholics have always rejoiced in the knowledge that no sinner is ever turned away from the Forgiveness of God and this is what they celebrate in the Sacrament of Reconciliation – in the Confessional.

Penance, Punishment & Repentance

The present notion regarding Evil, in that it describes wicked behaviour (breaking customary rules), is shared by all. All legal systems that we know about require the evil-doer to be punished. We are familiar with the 'Crime and Punishment' thing. . .it has been around since the beginning of time! While Christianity, with its admirable rules and regulations (p. 79), has kept its faithful people aware of the punishments due for Sin, with death as its ultimate punishment, it is nonetheless faced with the conundrum of God's forgiveness (p. 66). Christ's Death and Resurrection takes away the fear of death and points out, for each of us and for the community as a whole, the fulfilment of the Promise God made to Abraham. This was realized in the Christ who Himself promised life to the *repentant* sinner (*Luke* 23:43).

History is full of characters whose regret for past evil actions was seen in a change in their lifestyle. This would begin with a fast, or a severe course of physical privation. We find one notable Old Testament example of this sort of thing in the Story of Job. But in the early centuries of Christianity much was made of this behaviour. In fact, the public performance of rigorous privation was prescribed for serious Sin. . .and the death penalty for witchcraft, as well as for stealing and murder, was normal during the Middle Ages.

However, as the notion of God's Justice and Forgiveness began to take root, such penalties start to be replaced by more benign punishments. [In the second half of the twentieth century, as our civilization develops in the 'West', the Capital Penalty has mostly disappeared, except in some US states.]

One reason for this is the realization that the word 'Repentance' comes from the Greek expression for 'changing your mind'! It is not possible to change your way of life unless you first change your way of thinking about what your life means. Penance and Punishment had always to fit the *Crime*; it had nothing to do with the criminal as a Person. It is bad enough to be known as an Evil-doer without having to undergo a penalty for something that has happened, which cannot be undone!

We often hear it said: 'We now live in a "post-Christian world"'. However, our more civilized way of dealing with 'Sinners' tends to their rehabilitation – while they are persuaded to 'think again' about their behaviour – rather than their punishment. This though unrecognized, is, in fact, a highly Christianized attitude.

The West is slowly learning how to forgive. It will no doubt be centuries before we live in a Forgiving World. We can trace a development away from the earlier notion of the chain, which ran:- 'sin – punishment – repentance – reward' beginning with the sixth century BC prophet Ezekiel when he wrote that God said He 'wanted not the death of the sinner, but that he be converted and live'! (*Ezekiel* 18:32). People do not, as a rule, catch on particularly quickly. Almost two Chapters (5 & 6) of *St Paul's letter to the Romans* is devoted to this puzzle. . .and that was nearly 2,000 years ago! But, as we have to keep reminding ourselves – it's early days!

Like Christ, God-made-Man, who lived for a while in an inconsistent world so that Mankind could aim at something better, so the Catholic Church, as it has never failed to claim, assists Man in his efforts to achieve this destiny. To do this is only possible with God's help. None can doubt that human nature is sinful; nor can anyone quarrel with the Church's claims to exist for sinners. This is what justifies the Catholic Church's claim to follow Christ who came to call all sinners. We can see this from the later contributions to the New Testament.

In comparison with all that you have reflected upon in the Catholic Church's history since its beginning, it appears that the exclusiveness of Catholicism is gradually being reversed. . . but it's still early days!

6 Teachings [1] & Doctrines

Symbols of The Trinity

Understanding Death

'IN THE MIDST OF LIFE we are in death' cries the preacher. Every religious cult has centred on this conundrum. Since life is so precious to all living things, how is it that it comes to an end? For most of us 'death seems like a disaster'. We are reminded, too, of an earlier question: How is it that 'murder is a heinous crime' here, and yet 'ritual or judicial killing is a good thing' there? No doubt the strength of our instinct for self-preservation points to the preciousness of life, but in that case why is it that there is still no way in which life can be prolonged? Why should lives be spent

Christ being taken down from the cross ('The Deposition') - Pietro Lorenzetti (1305- 48), San Francesco, Assisi

avoiding death? However, as Christianity takes root this proverb gets reversed to read: 'In the midst of death we are in life!'

As a matter of interest, it is now generally agreed by scholars that no hope of individual survival after death is expressed in the Old Testament before some of its later passages which were written probably as late as the second century BC, and that previous cultures maintained a fatalistic attitude to life. Perhaps Israel's failure to reach a positive idea of 'survival after death' was partly due to its people's experience of Egyptian secularism. The people of Egypt, with whom the Israelites lived as an ethnic minority for some 400 years, felt that man's destiny was achieved in *this* life and was maintained, after death, in a twilight existence of material joy which would never change.

There is an evident striving for some form of 'afterlife' that can be seen in those of the Psalms (in the Bible dated around the seventh century BC) that ask for deliverance, from danger and death; this deliverance was seen as a privilege for those who keep God's laws. This would help to distinguish the righteous from the wicked as it is clear that the Psalmist saw death and destruction as punishment for God's enemies (the wicked). . . those who broke the Law.

It would not be profane to suggest here that it is from such ideas that we get the *formalized* idea of 'the bad versus the good' – with the bad always having to be punished and the good always rewarded. (See Ch. 5) Preservation from death would therefore be the lot of the righteous. But since everyone, then as now, good or bad, comes to the grave, the universality of death remained as much a problem for them as it has continued to be throughout the development of Man's history.

'What Can I Do For You?'

Having forgotten all about Good and Evil for the moment, you lean expectantly on the bar, approach the counter, answer the door-bell. The moment someone appears the first thing to be said is: 'Yes? What can I do for you?' In a moment you are dealing with someone who can help, and, whatever it happens to be, the business is transacted. It is all to do with 'service'. . . doing something for someone else. It is normal procedure and when it is done, one moves away to do something else. Constantly dealing with others, 'doing things for others', often leaves little time for oneself. Mothers with families usually find this to be so.

The whole of life is spent with others. So one finds that one of the tenets of Christianity (based in the Old Testament) is that we are to treat one another as we would like to be treated. . . with love. The Old Testament, however, sees God as paramount and orders that we *first* love God above all 'things' (presumably including 'persons'). Since no one can see God, that makes it rather difficult, so we tend to forget that particular order and concentrate on the Neighbour.

Nowadays, Christianity is seen less to be about God than about being kind to one another. We are told that love means 'caring and sharing' and as long as we do that 'we should do alright'! Folk seem not too keen on knowing much about God anyway. Islam has it that God/Allah cannot be known, so for Muslims the question is somewhat irrelevant.

'Dogma'/doctrine one can leave to others. And that is what we will do here and leave it for the moment.

□

Judaism in Old Testament times was not a 'credal' religion. As the Hebrews had no positive notion of an 'afterlife', 'Salvation' for them meant 'knowledge of the Law'! The Law was all that mattered, so Jewry, strictly speaking, did not need to have a Creed (a list of things to be believed) in addition to the Law even when Moses Maimonides produced one in Spain in the twelfth century AD. However, the Church, after generations of trying to deal with theological difficulties, definitively produced a Christian Creed in Constantinople in 381AD.

Maimonides may have had a memory of the time when Jewry was severely persecuted by the Catholic Church – he himself being chased for being a Muslim! The Christian Creed is not centred so much on dogmatic truths as is sometimes thought, but on what we know about God and about what He has done. The Dogma comes later.

The Trinity

By the end of the first century of the Christian era it had become clearer to believers that 'there are Three Persons in God'. This was called the 'Blessed Trinity'. No one knows how this should be. [Just as no one yet knows why it should take one million years for the temperature at the centre of the Sun to reach its surface, or why our distance from the Sun should be so critical, or yet how can bumblebees fly since, designwise, they are aerodynamic disasters, or how bees construct those perfect hexagonal prisms terminated by pyramids to house their eggs and honey. . . . (but remember it's early days!)]

We find that Early Christian writers were aware of the 'Trinity' from what they had learnt from the Christ. But as to its *meaning* the Bible is silent. It may well have been reflected in the Old Testament. References to an '*Angel* of God', ('*Angel* of the Lord', '*Spirit* of the Lord', '*Power* of the Highest', 'the lord God and His *Spirit*' etc.) pointed to beings distinct from God but those writers never thought of these beings, in any sense, sharing in God's Nature!

'God' is always outside our experience. We have probably recognized that by now. What we do know from experience is that everything there is, exists in some sort of relationship with something else. The lamp is on that table which is on the floor of a house in this street, in this town, in this county, in this country which is in this world which is part of the Milky Way, which is in this Galaxy, which is. . . etc., etc. Very often 'Gravity' and 'Light' demonstrate these relationships quite adequately. Since it seems to be impossible for anything in Nature to exist outside any sort of relationship, there is therefore no reason why there ought not also to be some sort of relationship between the Persons in the Blessed Trinity.

Hindsight has allocated 'Names' and 'Functions' to these Persons in an attempt to understand what is meant by 'The Trinity' and what might be the relationship between these Persons. The Trinity is beyond our experience. Some early Christians tried to use 'mythical'-type methods to expound it, and these gave rise to what were called 'heresies'. Nonetheless, we still have no adequate language to express this truth. We find the earliest formulation of it in the New Testament (at the end of Paul's Second Letter to the Christians in Corinth; and at the end of the Gospel which follows Matthew's tradition).

Both of these reflect early Christian traditions of performing the Rite of Baptism where 'one needs to confess this Faith'. Stated simply, we could express it as follows:-

• 1. God (the Father) Creator of the Universe with Man made in his Image: whether by a 'Big Bang' to start with or otherwise, it does not really matter.

• 2. God (the Son) appears in Time to resolve the difficulties Man has found for himself. This is the Jesus Christ who arrives at such a period, perhaps, when Man's ability to communicate had reached that point when such a Revelation would take root.

• 3. God (the Holy Spirit) is the Wisdom of God and also the Life Force, by which, down the centuries, this Revelation grows, in so many different ways, in the heart of Man.

These three Persons feature in the Apostle's Creed (opposite) which our children learn.

This credal formula reflects the tradition of the teaching of the Apostles (men who had met the Christ and who had been chosen by him to preach his Gospel) but the ideas contained in this Creed are too advanced to be attributable entirely to them. Later, the Roman Emperor Constantine, the one who lifted the persecution of the Christians and established Christianity as the State religion, called a Council meeting of all the Bishops in the Empire to meet in Nicaea (325AD) to affirm the Faith in the face of the 'Arian crisis'. (Arius was a priest from Alexandria who denied 'Christ is God' and his ideas became quite popular.)

The Apostle's Creed

'I believe in God, the Father Almighty, Creator of Heaven and Earth; and in Jesus Christ, his only Son, our Lord; who was conceived by the Holy Spirit, born of the Virgin Mary; suffered under Pontius Pilate, was crucified, dead, and buried; He descended into hell; the third day He rose again from the dead; He ascended into heaven; is seated at the right hand of God the Father Almighty; from thence He shall come to judge the living and the dead.

I believe in the Holy Spirit; the Holy Catholic Church: the Communion of Saints; the Forgiveness of Sins; the Resurrection of the Body; and Life everlasting. Amen.'

This Council at Nicaea produced the Nicene Creed which had a profound influence on other Baptism Creeds of the fourth century (so there were *other* Creeds already in use by then). After that, some others denied 'the Holy Spirit is God', so Constantine's successor, Emperor Theodosius I, called another Council which met at Constantinople in 381. This Council revised the work composed in 325 AD and produced the Creed with which modern Christians are most familiar.

Since 'misunderstanding' is something in which everyone seems to excel, it was vital that, to avoid any possibility of further error, they should try to get the words as right as possible! Which is probably why it has not been necessary to make any alterations (apart from what we find in the translations) since then.

7 'Judgement & Deliverance'

HINDSIGHT leads us to consider the Old Testament as being rather judgemental in the way it covers Hebrew history. There were rewards; but for those who broke the Law detailed punishments were prescribed. The Hebrews interpreted God's rules in terms of 'Retribution' – the penalties for breaking them. Many people still respond to any Rules in those terms. God's enemies were always seen as those opposed to his Chosen People, including enemies within; eventually they all came to a sticky end.

By way of another detour, it is worth mentioning

that 'Judgement' in the Old Testament has several other meanings. The Bible contains a Book, the *Book of Judges* which relates 12 stories of individual heroes, charismatic military-type leaders, who appear to have done some astonishing things during the initial period of the Hebrew occupation of the Canaanite country (dated possibly at the end of thirteenth and beginning of twelfth century BC). They were described as 'deliverers' rather than as those who sit in judgement and parcel out penalties for wrong-doing. Hence the *deliverance* of the Hebrew people from their slavery in Egypt under Moses was seen as a great act of Judgement on their God's part. Some translations miss this particular nuance which is unfortunate as the New Testament emphasizes Christ as being the 'deliverer', Saviour and Redeemer of his people from Sin rather than as a the Judge who condemns the wicked.

From Judgement to Forgiveness

In the New Testament we find this approach being developed further: Man has been elevated, as it were, to a 'higher plane' through the coming of the Christ. We saw, in the simple Creed (p. 63), that Christians believe in the 'Forgiveness of Sin'. Christ was recognized by John the Baptist as the one *'who takes away the sin of the world'*.[13] The Christ is shown as forgiving all Sin/wrongdoing, and his followers are expected to do the same. The Commandment 'Love your neighbour as yourself', an Old Testament precept that contained, in one principle, the meaning of the whole Hebrew Law and the Prophets, was now to be 'upgraded'. We are encouraged to love one another as the Christ loves us – seemingly by forgiving each other for the wrong, real or imagined, that is done to us.

Christ teaches *'A man can have no greater love than to lay down his life for his friends'*.[14] This is a statement of fact. . . but what does it mean? 'Laying down one's life' can hardly involve Death since death would put an end to the friendship! A soldier lays down his life for his friends when he *joins* the Army, not when he leaves it! In addition, it is meaningless to die for someone for whom you have not lived! Experience, therefore, seems to indicate that the most effective way one can demonstrate this 'greater love', in what has to be an on-going relationship, would be to 'forgive the friend' with a forgiveness, which, since this is a matter of love, would have to be **unconditional**.

Relief When We are 'Let Off'

It is generally recognized that being **'let off'** after having been caught in a misdemeanour, brings great relief. The relief experienced comes from realizing that some Punishment has been avoided. The more serious the offence and the more serious the penalty – the greater the relief! But being 'let off the punishment' does not remove the knowledge that one is 'guilty of the misdemeanour'. Even so, those five relieving words: *'If I catch you again'* will be sufficient, one hopes, to prevent a repetition of the wrong done. Being **Forgiven**, on the other hand, is more profound than being 'let off'. It goes far deeper even than any legal 'exoneration'. It is in the 'love situation' that forgiveness reaches this peculiar Mystery which, in some strange way, involves **'the restoration of my innocence'**.

We started with Judgement and end up speaking of Forgiveness – that can't be bad!

'Abuse' of Forgiveness?

This is one aspect of Catholicism that has been the cause of some dissension and resulted in the charge of hypocrisy. With the prospect of having one's sins forgiven, does this not open the door to the sort of licence which cannot be in the mind of a Church dedicated to the pursuit of virtue? . . . or to put it another way; 'Knowing that no one will be turned away, will not God's forgiveness surely be open to abuse?'

In providing this guide to Roman Catholicism, I was asked to avoid, as far as possible 'the spiritual dimension'. However, as 'forgiveness' is one of the very few spiritual experiences we are likely to recognize, perhaps we might have a moment to dwell on this aspect of Catholic teaching and practice.

As we belong in a material world, our experiences, even when they are merely emotional experiences, can be described in material terms and so a medical doctor would be able, often enough, to recognize the symptoms. Man does not naturally see his world in *spiritual terms*, so he is not used to having 'spiritual or religious experiences', and therefore it is highly unlikely for him to recognize one should it happen. Inevitably, such experiences are very infrequent. Consequently, whenever they have occurred down the ages, they have required prolonged examination by the Church before being judged to be authentic.

My '*feeling* that God has spoken to me', would be a *recognizable experience*. On the basis of 'feeling' I would then have to say that this experience was more likely to be of an emotional rather than a spiritual nature. The moment they can be 'felt' such experiences are normally described as emotional.

The Catholic Church is our only authority in such matters and it is from that authority that we learn of God's Forgiveness. Such forgiveness may well be accompanied by a feeling of elation and freedom with a heartfelt desire not to sin again. Even with a 'one off' firm purpose to amend one's life, experience has shown that these feelings are not usually sufficient to prevent any further wrongdoing. We know that God forgives Sin. Faith confirms this. And so that is really that! It is because of its *spiritual* nature that it is not open to physical experience. For this reason it is not open to abuse, nor, therefore, are those who confess their sins, in the Sacrament of Reconciliation, open to the charge of hypocrisy.

Restoration of Innocence

The Forgiveness of God bears little if any resemblance to the manner in which we forgive one another. When you forgive someone you tend to expect the other not to commit the same offence again. Often enough, it will be a forlorn hope. However, when God forgives, it is total and unconditional; it is a perfect Act of Reconciliation. In human terms (which are themselves very limited) it is almost as though it (my sin) never happened, which is why I might describe God's forgiveness in terms of a *Restoration of my Innocence*.

However, that sort of forgiveness seems to be too much to ask of me! After all, none of us can claim to be this Christ. It is worth remembering that it is not possible to do what God wants unless, of course, one has some idea of who God is. That surely would be a matter of common sense. We must ask in order to receive; search in order to find. . . 'For the one who asks always receives; the one who searches always finds; the one who knocks will always have the door opened to him. Is there any among you who would hand a child a stone when he asked for bread? Or hand him a snake when he asked for a fish?' (*Matthew 7:7-11*).

The question then is: 'If we who are evil, know how to give our children what is good, how much more will our heavenly Father give good things to those who ask him?' [I apologize for quoting the Scriptures here. Sometimes it is useful – but not always. I was told once by someone that he had given up reading the Bible 'because he got bored with all the quotations!']

Who is to Judge?

To conclude this section on Forgiveness we might look at another question: 'Since God is Law-maker and therefore Judge how is it that He takes away the Sins of the world? Surely God should punish wrongdoing'. Nor is it strange that while '*I* want to be forgiven' – I still think all the other wrongdoers should be punished somehow![15]

Laws are *passed* by government and *administered* by the judiciary. Our present legal system is based largely on *Roman* law. The Bible (*Book of Judges*) gives us another idea of what Judgement means in *Hebrew* terms. As far as the Hebrew knows, God does not use the Roman way of administering Justice. As far as *we* know, God does not use the Hebrew way either. All we can say so far is that: *No one judges as God does.* Catholics are encouraged to take that statement on board before they start examining what they think about God's Justice! Many still think of God's Justice in Roman terms. Some even look for the time when all evil-doers 'go to Hell'!

A Judge in Court, upon hearing the Defendant clearing himself with: 'As God is my judge, I'm innocent!', declared hotly: 'He's not; I am and you aren't! – 20 days!'

We have only this world's standards against which to judge anything. Human standards are not always adequate. It would be unjust, therefore, to use merely human standards to judge the Catholic Church. A brief look at the ways political systems have changed down the centuries (choose whatever nation you will), and the wars which have resulted from such changes, should show the spiritual advantage the Church has over them.

'All wars are caused by religion' is a saying often quoted by those who wish to contribute to this discussion. It is plainly correct to say that wars are often caused by people who think and believe different things. The American humorist, James Thurber, however, was heard to remark that 'the trouble with the world is not that a lot of people *believe* different things – but that the different things they *believe* just aint so!' It is true to say, however, that in the past the Church has involved the civil arm of the law in order to deal harshly with those who appeared to have sought, tooth and nail, to destroy it, as we have seen (p. 26).

8 Myths

The Flood

Myths

ALL CIVILIZATIONS originally rejoiced in extensive Mythologies. Those of the Near East have now been largely recovered. Partly known since 1929 through surviving documents of ancient Ugarit languages, they illuminate many Old Testament allusions. They certainly show up the differences between ancient Canaanite mythological thinking and the religious thinking of neighbouring Israel. Many scholars had long agreed that no mythology was to be found in the Old Testament. But to *deny* mythology in the Old

Testament would leave a number of biblical passages without any satisfactory explanation. We ought not to dismiss the idea of 'myths' while we are trying to explain it!

Definition of a Myth:

A 'myth' is a traditional story which usually involves supernatural or imaginary persons. . .or both. It attempts to explain contemporary ideas of the Universe. Myths appear extremely distorted to us nowadays; but we need to recognize that this distortion is not necessarily due to mythological 'thinking' itself, any more than any errors in 'thinking' are due to the nature of the 'thinking' behind them. The scientist's calculations are correct, and they have been checked; but his conclusions are found to be wrong only because there was a distortion in the material on which he was working.

Those who would deny or debunk 'myth' usually measure it against their own standards of reasoning and so will obviously find 'myth' wanting. But in those cultures with little reasoning ability, mythological thinking is the *only* means for rationalizing problems for which there is no reason. 'Myth' *tries* to make 'intelligible' real experiences for which they had no adequate explanation. For example: if a particular day has to be extended so that a victory can be won in a battle, the easiest way is to show that the sun stood still! (*Joshua* 10:10ff) 'Why not?' asks our ancient chronicler, 'we see it travel regularly across the sky from dawn to dusk – why can't it be made to stop for us?' They will, of course, arrange for God to fix this for them!

It will not be long before this sort of notion affects

emerging science, which will later declare, without doubt, that the Sun goes round the Earth! Because of this sort of thing, modern analysis of the nature of 'myth' suggests that it is not the 'myth' that is false, but the observable facts that it represents.

Again, without an adequate understanding of the nature of things, how does one answer questions that have always interested Man? Since no one with a knowledge of science was there at the Beginning, or stood behind the fellow with the pen who wrote it down, how does one explain the Origin of the World and of Man? or, for that matter, What is the relationship of Man to Nature, or of Man to God? How do you know that you are a Person? or, Where did 'Society' come from? Nowadays, such problems can be approached with modern reasoning which has its own methods and principles; reasoning that is set to work on verifiable facts.

While 'Myth' deals with 'facts', verified or not, it does not really solve such questions, but *does* express the attitude that primitive Man takes in the presence of what he *thinks* is mysterious. That remark might be very enlightening, but it still remains questionable as to whether our discursive reasoning, with all its methods and principles, achieves any more than 'myth' does!

9 Faith & Morals

St Michael – triumphant over the Devil

THE HEBREWS did have problems about Faith! They knew that there was only one God, but somehow that was not enough for them. In the early days, if this God did not do what they expected of Him, they would complain. Like their surrounding neighbours they wanted God to fit in with *their* idea of a god! 'What do we have gods for anyway?' their neighbours would say; 'If they're no good – replace them!'

One finds this attitude from time to time, even nowadays. After a particularly nasty disaster you are quite likely to hear: 'I don't believe in a God who can allow that sort of thing to happen'. 'You can keep Christianity – the Church never got me anywhere!' There are no answers glib or otherwise that will help here. For those who *do* believe, of course, the question does not arise and so no answers are necessary. For those who do *not* believe no satisfactory answers are possible!

Aristotle's 'First Cause'

Though we now have a fair idea of what God is not, *we have no idea of what God is!* Aristotle (a Greek philosopher of the fourth century BC) on whose wisdom much of our modern thinking depends, was 90 before he was able to arrive at the existence of one such Being . . . that was the First Cause . . . but that it was beyond anything Man might experience. Thomas Aquinas (1225-74) arguably the genius towering over Catholic religious thought from then on, was only four when he asked: 'What is God?'

When we were kids we used to lie on the grass and watch the ants doing what ants do and marvelled at their industry. 'They can't see – yet they're very well organized.' It was clear that they had no idea about us! If you were to put an ant-sized man down there with them the ants would be unlikely to know what it was. Yet the ants are much closer to us than we are to this God of ours.

We have recently discovered that the diameter of the planet Rigal is larger than the diameter of the Earth's Orbit round our Sun! Somehow or other this

God has something to do with that, and with the existence of the ants, and everything in between. How this God got around to enter into this world of ours, dressed as a Common Man, we do not know. All we do know is that He did.

In some strange way, it was Something that the Hebrews expected though none of them knew how or when it would happen. The Jewish Scriptures which Christians have always accepted as 'kosher' are concerned with nothing other than the Coming of the Holy One who would take to Himself a People and make them His own. Faith is a special way of 'knowing' this to be true.

But as everyone who has been to school will say, and we have said it before: 'What's the point of knowing something if you can't use it?'. So Faith cannot be just a way of 'knowing'. It must be about '*being*'. Faith is about 'being a Christian'. [We have to be careful in the way we use <u>words</u> – because words are all we have in order to communicate with one another.] Christians tell us that Faith is a gift of God because without it Christians would not know who or what they were talking about! There is only one Faith and it comes to us in an extraordinary variety of ways. There are many religions in the world but there is only one Faith. This is why it is not accurate to say that we live in a 'multi-faith' environment. 'Multi-religion' or even 'Multi-culture' – yes; but 'Multi-faith' – no!

When we get to Catholicism we have gone as far as we can go – if we are talking about going anywhere! We spoke about the relationship the Hebrew people experienced with their God. This God made a Promise that He would arrange for the

Hebrew people to become a great Nation. But they had no idea how this was to be achieved. Christianity, as the successor to Judaism, with which it shares this destiny, recognizes that this great Nation is still beginning to appear. . . . this development is still beginning. Hindsight shows us that, as far as we know, it will always be – beginning!

☐

The 'Faith Journey'

We have learnt that the Bible traces the development of the Hebrew idea of God and His Creation and the Promises made to the Patriarchs. Science tells us that this probably took very much longer than we were led to believe. So it seems that Time means very little when one is speaking about 'God' – and His Work, and no matter how much of a mess we might make of the world and how we live in it . . . everything will work out in accordance with God's Will . . . and it will always be beginning . . . and most would agree that 'all change is a new becoming'.

'*The people that walked in darkness have seen a great light; on those who live in deep shadow a light has shone*' is a Scriptural expression (*Isaiah* 9:1) which would be as close as one could get to describing Faith. Christians will sometimes talk of a 'Faith journey' – a journey in time to a destiny to which we all look forward and in which we all hope. The importance of Authority, however, will be recognized the moment difficulties appear, that people seem to have in following the signs along the route.

Recognizing 'Truth'

In passing, one might say that Faith is not something *imposed* from outside, or something one needs in order to pass exams. It is a recognition of something 'mystic and wonderful' – that can be recognized as Truth. A list of its basic tenets was given earlier (p. 63), a set of basic principles that we can hold on to. They give a structure to Christianity – to prevent the faint-hearted from falling back into the superstitions to which all are prone. Again, it is much easier to say what Faith is *not* rather than to describe what it is. It is rather like life – it is easier to say what life is *not*. Trying to describe what life *is* becomes a little too personal for comfort.

Christians have inherited the Hebrew beginnings and have witnessed its development down the centuries. It is Faith that enables Catholics to say this with conviction.

If it is possible to make mistakes in our dealings with one another whom we can see, then it is easy enough to be mistaken when trying to see the path that the unseen God has laid out for us. A recognizable Authority *must* be on hand to clear up any difficulties that arise. So far, the Catholic Church is the only organization – notwithstanding the mistakes of the past and present – that claims to be 'It'. Catholics believe in God. . . . they also believe in the Catholic Church. This was written into that list of tenets mentioned earlier and nothing of such a nature seems to have happened in the interim as to require this tenet to be altered.

In the mind of the early Church it was not possible to believe in God without believing in the Catholic Church. Having spoken at some length about the phenomenon of Jesus Christ there is something in that notion which is still true. . . and provides yet another reason why Catholics say that there is only one Faith – and that all the other 'cults' are better described as 'confessions', 'cultures' 'professions', 'religions', 'traditions', – etc.

Morals

It is within living memory that people were heard to observe that Catholicism was to be admired because of the authority of its Church and the discipline of its members. The temptation, for Catholics, was to take a certain delight in this recognition. The truth of the matter, however, is more pedestrian. All Christian rules were inherited from Jewish traditions. The word 'orthodox', a Greek expression for 'sound doctrine', is taken nowadays to indicate one who observes the official or authorized teachings of the community to which he or she belongs.

By the time of Christ, many of the rules regarding orthodox Jewish religious observance were old by many centuries. Some of them, however, were given short shrift by the early Christians – namely the importance of Circumcision, the strict Observance of the food laws, and, later, Attendance at the Temple or the Synagogue. The rules governing daily life remained to be kept as they still are. The Book of the Covenant (*Exodus*), in which one finds 'The Decalogue' (Ten Comandments) was composed against a background of numerous law codes of the ancient Near East, perhaps the earliest, written in Sumerian, dates from about 2050BC.

The most famous of the ancient Near Eastern cuneiform codes is that of a Mesopotamian chieftain,

Hammurabi, who ruled the Amorite dynasty 1728-1686BC. With the discovery of his code in 1901, (p. 39) it became evident that ancient Mesopotamian legislation had long provided for practically every detail of the life-situation described in *Genesis*. A later Hittite Code (about 1450BC) has preserved some 200 laws.

Just as the Hebrews were influenced by and assimilated the laws of the country they invaded (Palestine-Canaan), so Christianity drew upon the laws of Judaism. Since the same God is worshipped by both traditions, the rules concerning all moral behaviour continued throughout the transformation and beyond. ['The Decalogue' includes anti-pagan adjustments in the prologue as worship of the one God was now prescribed.]

God and the Neighbour

The Hebrews believed: 'Our Law is the Law of God'. The meaning of the Old Testament Law and the Prophets was summed up in the precept: '*You must love God above all things and your neighbour as yourself.*'[16] One's behaviour towards God and towards the Neighbour (p. 59) were therefore not to be separated. Though it was understood that the one involved the other, the Hebrew's duty to God was always first and foremost.

But how long did it take for the Hebrews to arrive at the notion that their worship of God was inseparable from their duty to a Neighbour? It clearly arose from their attitude to the Law. But what is strange, especially with hindsight is that, what began as an acculturation with a contemporary *pagan* code of ethics should become incorporated with something so sacred to the Hebrews as the Word of God. Is this why it was another 300 years (we take the archaeological arguments for dating the Exodus) to the time of the Kings, before the Ten Commandments were committed to writing?

Whatever answer we have for this, *Mark 12:29*, with its parallel passages in the other Gospel accounts, provides us with the first expression in the Bible of both these precepts being pronounced as one. [This also suggests that by the time *Mark's Gospel* was written this thinking was already traditional among Jews.] Christianity has made much of this, and it is oddly recognized in such often-heard comments as: 'You don't have to go to church to be a good Christian' – or – 'To see the awful way those people behave and to think they're all church-goers!'

The 'Morals' Debate

Europe in the Middle Ages enjoyed such pastimes as 'Debating'. These intellectual exercises were designed not only to improve the mind, but also to plumb those truths which had long been the province of superstition and in which 'myth' was largely employed. The Greeks and Romans had engaged in similar exercises and their books demonstrate the conclusions that they reached. The *Book of Job* (composed between the sixth and seventh centuries BC) would be a good example of debate in the Old Testament. One such medieval debate centred on such questions as this: 'Are Morals possible *without* Religion?' For obvious reasons the answer has to be either 'Yes' or 'No'.

Simply stated, those who say 'Yes' deny themselves the privilege of having an Absolute against which to measure the rightness of a course of action and are thereby restricted to base their judgements merely on human expediency. Pagan systems worked very well in this way, but ultimately much of their decision-making was undertaken on the advice of Sibyls and Seers whose authority was accepted without question. Julius Caesar was told to 'Beware of the Ides of March' – had he lived to tell the tale, that Seer might well have met the same fate! (Such was the grip of superstition on the pagan mind in those days!) People still seek such advice from Astrologers and Horoscopes. Saul and Macbeth may be names which spring to mind and, of course, there are many others.

Those who say 'No' and accept the Absolute against which to measure the rightness (moral value) of a course of action, have the problem of coping with what appears to be the unfairness of the human condition. While they do not seem to 'worry' about deciding how to cope with all the exceptions to the law, they have to put up with all those who, understandably, consider them to be heartless and inhuman.

The 'Absolute' to which we have referred in this case is God. Now if we consider 'religion' to be a merely private affair then the 'Yes' group is right. However, 'orthodoxy' teaches us that one's duty to God and Neighbour are inseparable, and since the Neighbour is in the public sector, this would prompt one to answer 'No'.

The principles of moral conduct, as proposed by the Catholic Church for universal acceptance has scarcely changed since the early days. Most principles have been explained and adjusted in accordance with the developing needs of the people.

They, like the Decalogue, are couched in terms that involve 'human rights'. We all have 'rights' in tune with the human nature which God has given us. These 'rights' *belong* to us as Persons having been made in God's Image.

What Rights?

The Church is careful to distinguish 'rights' that are *recognizably* God-given from those 'rights' that are *assumed* to be God-given. The fact that some people might want something as of 'right' does not thereby make it a 'right'. If 'something' is not already true, our *believing* it to be true will not thereby make it true! There are plenty of problems nowadays concerning human rights and no amount of private thinking or opinion will solve them.

A large poster on the workshop wall proved helpful to all the mechanics in the garage. It read: 'When you have any problems always consult the Manufacturer's Handbook!'

10 Practices

Jesus – the 'Lamb of God'

THIS GUIDE began with a few thoughts about a primitive herdsman who depended totally on some god or other, and how he would 'pray' or 'sacrifice something valuable' in order to get this god to do what he wanted. In order to achieve some sense of security – as in our dealings with our neighbours, where a 'gift' always softens the hardest heart, 'sacrificing to a god' is no different. While the tribesman may be considered very primitive, man since his earliest years has been a 'sacrificing being'.

Since the Jewish Scriptures aim to describe the

Celebration of Holy Mass

unfolding relationship between God and his chosen People, Old Testament writers never fail to mark the highlights in their stories with some form of action at an 'altar'. Way back in the Bronze Age, a thousand years before it was ever called 'Passover', Hebrews held a sacrifice of lambs. It was in the Spring, and celebrated the return of life after the Winter dark. Much later, the Israelites, turned this into a Thanksgiving and Communion sacrifice in celebration of their miraculous escape from 400 years of Egyptian slavery (the 'Passover', or 'Exodus', in Moses' time).

Sacrifice

Sacrifice is first mentioned in *Genesis* with the Cain & Abel story. It is written in a way that suggests that there was already, by then, a tradition of sacrifice in place. The practice of 'present-giving' – 'presentation of gifts' to mark some important occasion has long been a habit in the Western world. In fact, it is a universal procedure and the reasons behind it are the same the world over. The Old Testament *Book of Leviticus* gives lengthy details as to the manner in which their different religious sacrifices were to be performed.

From the tenth century BC, when the Israelite Jerusalem Temple was built, all sacrifices were held there rather than on the traditional make-shift altars on hilltops. As they became a settled pastoral people, by the seventh century BC, the recalling of the Passover (from Egyptian slavery) had become linked to a Canaanite agricultural feast which marked the ripening of the barley. The Hebrews called their celebration the *Azymes*, or the Feast of 'Unleavened Bread'.

The Covenant with Abraham (p. 29) was to be repeated in different ways as the Hebrew mind-set developed. Later thinking will produce a ritual that would express the need for man's cooperation.[17] Man's gradual involvement in the Covenant will be seen in the development of a series of Laws (many taken from neighbouring cultures) the promulgation of which was marked by a Ritual.

After writing down all these commands (now attributed to Yahweh) and reading them to the waiting crowd, a *'communion sacrifice'* took place. The ritual was highly symbolic. By Moses' authoritative decree the victim's blood became the *symbol* of the Covenant: a symbol which not only 'made present' again the Covenant, but now included those rules that Hebrews kept to make them recognizable as God's People. [This synthesis took generations to develop from Abraham's day. It will not be until the fifth century BC that we will find it written into the works of the Hebrew 'New Age' desert travellers around 1300BC.]

With the Temple's Destruction (70AD) and the cessation of its special function of 'Sacrifice', Christians needed to develop a ritual on the lines of a 'temple-like' activity. Remember, please, that Christianity is a development of the Jewish pattern of life and as it grew out and away from its predecessor, hindsight shows that it was important for them not to lose those ties which were considered vital.

The Eucharist

Moving up another 500 years we see the pattern of Christian life gradually emerging, with its elements of prayer, mission and alms-giving. These elements could well be spoken of in such sacrificial terms as 'greater love than this has no man but that he lay down his life for a friend' (p. 66). The early Church had witnessed the destruction of the Temple and was now looking for its own *Ritual Sacrifice* that would reflect these elements.

The *Eucharist* – a Greek word for 'thanksgiving' – had gradually adjusted the notion of the 'Breaking of Bread' from a memorial ritual (not only to recall the Hebrew Passover but now in memory of the Last Supper when Christ had Broken the Bread) until it could also embrace the notion of Sacrifice.

Human culture, since its beginnings, has generally held the death of a victim to be the highest, the capital form of surrender – a *sign* of willing dependence. As civilizations develop and move away from the pagan ritual of 'human sacrifice' this *sign* has tended to be replaced by gifts of farm animals or produce. But it has been part of Western culture since Roman times, to consider the loss-of-one's-life-for-a-cause as '*the supreme sacrifice*'.

Resurrection

By a curious turn of events, beyond the scope of this book to chart in detail, the Christ, who came to fulfil the Promise of the Covenant and all the later prophecies that repeat it, is rejected by his own people and executed – we are told – for blasphemy! So he is put to death for a Jewish Cause: which, in the Hebrew mind-set of the time, was the protection of their heritage. The Christ had blasphemed their Temple! In the Christian mind-set, his death was not just the vindication of the Hebrew tradition of killing their prophets but the ushering-in of the great event of the Resurrection. The Passion narratives, in the Gospel stories, recount the story of his Death and also his Resurrection, as well as his subsequent appearances to some of his friends.

The Hebrew tradition expected the ninth century BC prophet, Elijah, to return to his people *during a meal*, so Christians expected the now Risen Christ to appear during a meal. You can read how all the appearances of Christ to his friends after the Resurrection take place during a meal. However, it will take another 1000 years in the Christian era before both these notions, the supreme sacrifice of Jesus Christ on the Cross *and* his Presence at a meal, will be seen as essential elements in the Eucharist and be accepted *universally* as such among Christians.

Holy Mass

In the traditions of the Roman Catholic and Eastern Churches, this is called the Holy Mass: it is not a 'repetition' of what took place in the Upper Room, rather it makes 'present again' the Last Supper shared by Jesus Christ with his disciples. As Jews, many early Christians went to the Temple for their sacrificial worship; and after that they would meet, in private with their Christian friends, for the Eucharist. Thus, they would not have associated the Eucharist with 'Temple sacrifice'. It was only after the sacrificial activity of the priests had been discontinued with the destruction of the Temple, that any 'priestly' language was taken over by Christians and used for the Eucharist – or 'the Breaking of Bread' as they called it.

While all that seems to be fairly straightforward, it will not be long before some people will start finding fault with the language used to describe the Eucharist, (as we will see later with the Iconoclasts) and begin to deny certain aspects of the Church's teaching regarding the manner of Christ's Presence; they will also quarrel with certain notions concerning the sense in which the Eucharist is a Sacrifice.

Every attempt of the Church to apply *reasoning* to these questions, for the benefit of the curious, often made their solutions appear more difficult. The philosophical approach to the problem known as 'Transubstantiation', introduced into Church teaching during the Council of Trent (1543-63), while satisfying the majority, only served to anger those who had made up their minds to reject it 'because such an idea was not to be found in the Bible'.

The 'Sacrifice' of the Mass

'Sacrifice', vital in esxpressing Man's total dependence on his Deity, is part of every generation's religious activity. Catholics see their Mass in these terms, which is why they accept the obligation to attend (however shaky their personal beliefs might be), and to participate in this ritual each Sunday, the 'first day of the week', the day on which Jesus Christ, God-the-Son, rose from the dead for the sake of our world.

☐

Sundays and Holy Days

Sundays and great Feast Days in the Catholic Church are Holy Days – from which word we get 'Holiday'. We tend not to remember that, in England, the English language developed during a period of almost 1000 years up to the time of the Reformation, in a highly Catholicized atmosphere. Every aspect of human experience was seen in religious terms. All Church festivals were celebrated with glee in much the same way as our Jewish ancestors did when they took over the Pagan Festivals and *mores* which had already existed for centuries (p. 21). Christians did the same (there not being much point in changing the *dates*) and transformed them into a celebration of Christ's presence.

Thus, the pagan Festival of the 'Coming of the Light to end the Darkness of Winter' became the Festival of **Christmas** the 'Coming of the Christ, the Light of the World'. [Those living in the 'northern hemisphere' having no idea of the existence of rest of the world, were not aware that, in the 'southern hemisphere', the seasons of Winter and Summer are reversed.]

While the Jewish Sabbath (Saturday: when all Jews were commanded to rest) recalled the rest God himself took on completing of his Creation as noted in *Genesis*, this was superseded by Christians with the **Sunday** (in Jewish usage the 'First day of the Week') in accordance with the Gospel tradition, since this is the day the Christ Rose from the Dead. [Hebrews date the Sabbath at the 'end' of the week; the Christians will have the important day at the 'beginning' of the week.] Apart from Christmas, there are other important 'days'.

Strangely enough (because it is a Jewish ritual), Catholics celebrate Christ's Circumcision. This is celebrated at the **Epiphany**, the Feast of the Three Wise Men (6 January), because it was at that moment that Simeon, the first to do so, recognized this Child as the Fulfilment of the Promise that God had made to Abraham. '**Palm Sunday** of the Passion of the Lord' (as it is now called) recalls Christ's triumphal entry into Jerusalem and begins 'Holy Week' during which Catholics recall Christ's Last Supper, his Arrest and Execution. **Good Friday**, because of the Crucifixion (the manner of his execution), has been a day of mourning since the earliest days of the Church. **Easter Sunday** commemorates his Rising from the Dead.[18] The earliest Christian tradition maintained that the Christ had remained here, after his Resurrection, for a further 40 days; hence his **Ascension** into Heaven is celebrated about 40 days after Easter.

Other Feast Days

Moving away from celebrating events in the life of Christ, Catholics enjoy the Feast of '**Corpus Christi**' ('The Body of Christ') which celebrates the Eucharist as our spiritual Food. The Scripture readings for the Feast recall the Old Testament Covenant, the Feeding of the Hebrews as they wandered in the Desert during the Exodus and Christ's Feeding of the 5,000 (*John's Gospel* Ch. 6). **The Feast of SS Peter and Paul** (29 June) celebrates the two main characters who headed the Christian Mission in its beginnings. Both are thought to have been martyred in Rome during the 60s.

The Assumption of Our Lady into Heaven (15 August) is a celebration of the dignity traditionally accorded to the Blessed Virgin Mary. Christians have always held that, as Mother of Christ, she was without sin, and therefore strictly speaking, did not die (since death has always been considered to be the result of sin) but was taken up into Heaven when her time in this world had expired.

We all know the Feast of **All Saints**. The Medieval 'Hallowe'en' is the vigil of, or evening before, 'All Hallows', our All Saints Day (1 November). Here we celebrate the destiny of Mankind in the Communion of Saints which belongs among the last tenets of Faith listed in the Apostle's Creed (p. 63).

□

Other Catholic Practices

With all that has gone before, with the centuries it has taken for the official teachings of the Church to develop, the manner in which Catholics have practised their religion has also changed in some directions.

When Berengarius and some of his friends in the eleventh century denied Christ's Presence in the Eucharist, the Church was prompted to institute a little ceremony known as '**Benediction**' – a service of Reparation to God for this and other dishonours shown to the Eucharist (by then universally accepted as *the* sign of Christ's Presence). It took the form of the Sacred Wafer (the Consecrated Bread) being placed in a glass receptacle (called a Monstrance) so as to be seen and worshipped by the congregation. It took nearly 400 years for the service of 'Benediction' to become a worldwide practice.

As the Faith gradually spread, further develop-ments in Catholic devotion appeared. For example, '**The Holy Rosary**', a devotion that meditates on the mysteries of Christ's Birth, Death and Resurrection and the place the Virgin Mary took throughout, is centred on 1) the 1st Chapter of the Gospel according to Luke which relates the words the Angel

Gabriel and, later, her cousin Elizabeth addressed to her, and on 2) the Passion narratives and on the period following the Resurrection. This practice dates from the twelfth century and is attributed to St Dominic who also founded a religious Order of Preachers.

Though Friday is the traditional day on which Christ was put to death, the practice of going to Mass on the **First Friday** of every month did not become popular until the eighteenth century.

Most Catholic churches have 14 pictures adorning the walls – pictures depicting, in stages, the **Way of the Cross**. The ancient practice is to spend a while before each picture, or 'Station', to remind oneself, of the sufferings of Christ before his death on Mount Calvary. It has become fashionable, recently, to add a 15th 'Station' to celebrate his Resurrection. This devotion is usually performed during the six weeks of Lent, a period during the Church's year when Christians prepare for Easter, the Day on which Christ rises from the Dead.

Just as it is customary nowadays for crowds to process with their banners and national flags to mark a special occasion, there has always been the localized practice of carrying round, in **Processions** statues of Mary, or one of the Saints to whom this or that community is dedicated, and these have been fashionable for generations. There are many other similar traditions which are practised by Catholics to remind themselves of their religious inheritance and they are often performed in answer to some need or other.

11 Teachings [II] & Doctrines

The Lion & Gospel of St Mark

As WE HAVE SEEN, Judaism in Old Testament times was not a 'credal' religion. But it did have its laws (The Decalogue given to Moses), which, by the time of Christ, had grown to over 600 ordinances. These dealt both with religious observance and day-to-day dealings with one's Neighbour. As Christianity grew away from Judaism some of the specifically Jewish religious precepts were discarded but most of the neighbourly rules were kept.

For Hebrews, remembering the dynamic aspects of the Egyptian way of life which they shared, a life of wealth in this world was seen as a presage of wealth in the next life; and each Jew was born to it! However, for Jews who believed in Jesus, eternal happiness depended instead on belonging rather to God's family. This meant that one's earthly condition played little part in what happened beyond the grave. Even so, the ideal for the early Church was to raise the level of the poor, and to do this 'all goods were to be held in common' so as to distribute their surplus more easily. Apart from this there appear to have been no moral principles that distinguished Christian *mores* from the earlier Hebrew culture. This is understandable enough since the first Christians were themselves Jews.

Responding to the Commandments

The Moral teachings of the Catholic Church down the ages can still be seen to be grounded in The Decalogue. Each generation has brought with it its own difficulties. The abuse of power and of human rights is endemic to the human condition. It is not the aim here to sit in judgement on the way in which we deal with moral difficulties, past or present. That might best be left to chroniclers, artists and cartoonists whose work has reflected the besetting 'problems' of their day. The present symptom of 'sex & violence', though perhaps temporary, is nonetheless worrying; as each 'problem', in its own way, is but a contravention of these Commandments.

The normal impression we get is that these Commandments are honoured more in their breach than in their observance. What remains extremely interesting is that no one has ever seriously thought of adjusting them to suit prevailing fashions (and by 'prevailing' I mean 'down the ages'!)

The Apostle's Creed (p. 63) was described as the basic structure on which all Faith rests. Since it took some 300 years to produce, it will not be long before someone asks: 'Why was there a delay?'. We can chance one reply: Judaism had no Creed. For the Jews belief in God was accommodated by their knowledge of their Laws which had been well promulgated. There was, therefore, no argument indicating that Christianity, being a development of Judaism, should have a Creed. The Hebrews had no arguments. Their rules were cut and dried. However, many of these regulations were done away with once Christianity began to pull away from Jewish traditions.

Greek Philosophy, which had tried in vain to influence Jewish thought, played havoc with the preaching of the early Church and sought to dismiss the truth of Christ's Resurrection. Added to this, the efforts to justify the authority with which the Gospel was preached, produced problems that required the sort of solutions that would silence those who tried to use the Scriptures to counteract their success.

Those opposing the Church's missionary work would say that if a notion is not to be found in the Scriptures it could not be true. What the Church was now teaching was not readily available for them in the New Testament. What caused further difficulty for many Jews who had come to believe in Christ was that some of the traditional Jewish strictures had been cancelled. They had a memory of Christ saying that *'Not one dot nor one little stroke shall disappear from the Law until its purpose is achieved'*. (*Matthew's Gospel* 5:18). It was difficult for them to recognize that, in Christ, the purpose of the Law had been fulfilled! For many Christians it is still difficult.

To be fair, it is clear, from the later parts of the New Testament, that the early preachers did go beyond what Jesus Christ taught. This can be seen in the way John, Paul and Luke, the first missionaries, related to the Samaritans and to the Gentiles (pagan people who as yet had no idea of Christ's existence). Some of these developments took place within a generation! Since that was the case in the early days, a fair amount of Catholic teaching will be seen to go beyond what is to be found in the New Testament. One notable divergence from Jewish embargoes was the emergence of Icons.

The Iconoclasts & the Eucharist

The Iconoclasts – those who did not like Icons (painted images and statues) – had their moment in the eighth and ninth centuries. The first of the Ten Commandments reads: *You shall not make yourself a carved image or any likeness of anything in heaven or on the earth beneath or in the waters under the earth; you shall not bow down to them or serve them* (p. 40). While the wording of this Commandment might be ambiguous, it has always been a human practice to make representations or symbols of important figures to promote their memories for subsequent generations and even use them in teaching those not able to read (p. 120). But apart from the story of the Brazen Serpent (*Book of Numbers: Ch. 21*) there is no evidence of the Hebrews making religious images *after* the promulgation of the Commandments. Indeed, the superstitious adulation or worship of such icons, thus turning them into Idols, has always been considered reprehensible by Judaism, Christianity and Islam alike.

Moses used animal blood to *symbolize* the

Covenant, and animal sacrifices were performed to 'make present' again God's Promise thus reminding the people of their special status. So the tradition of using symbols was part of Hebrew culture. However, in early Christian language such terms as 'symbol', 'figure' were used in relation to the Eucharist (p. 87). If to symbolize a 'Promise' (Covenant) poses no difficulty; why not symbolize a 'Presence'. . . recalling Christ's Presence during a meal by Breaking the Bread? No problem there.

Unfortunately, the words 'icon' and 'type', introduced by those with an eastern approach to the subject, compounded the difficulty they had of finding the right expressions that would satisfy the desire to *describe* the Real Presence of Christ. 'But since Christ is really present in the Eucharist then surely there can be no room for such representative expressions.' [It is confusing in the extreme to suggest that the 'Reality' is really just a 'Symbol of that Reality'!]

The resulting bewilderment produced a serious problem when they came to develop an understanding of the Eucharist as *Christ's Sacrifice*! The solution was to get rid of the symbols altogether. The opponents of Images argued, among other things, that the Church has no need of paintings of Jesus Christ since she already possessed his Image in the Eucharist. On the strength of this the Iconoclasts held a synod in Constantinople in 754 to authorize the destruction of the Icons.

So important was it to find a solution to this impasse that another meeting, the 7th Ecumenical Council of Nicaea (787), took place to restore them; and so today, as has been the case since that time, the Eastern Churches, (Catholic, in practically everything

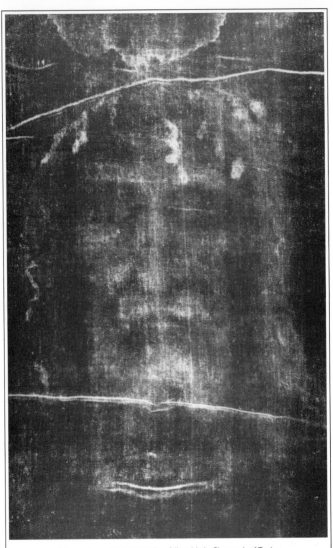

Negative photograph of the Holy Shroud of Turin

we have discussed, except that they are not in union with Rome), make much use of Icons in the design of their churches and Liturgy.

The Holy Shroud of Turin

The most celebrated Christian image is the Holy Shroud of Turin, a piece of linen reputed to be the burial cloth in which the mangled body of Jesus Christ was laid to rest.

Eastern Orthodox Christians have always thought artistic pictures of Christ were based on a mysterious image of Jesus on a cloth which they called the Mandylion. It is thought that this Mandylion cloth was taken from Byzantium, early in the thirteenth century, strangely coinciding with an 'unknown' period of the Shroud's history. It had surfaced, in the sixth century in Edessa in Eastern Turkey, after an earlier period of disappearance.

There is evidence that the Mandylion and the Shroud could be one and the same, though no one suggested this at the time. There is a striking similarity between the full face of Jesus on copies of the Mandylion, and what an early artist might make of the face on the Shroud.

Recent controversy that resulted in the Shroud being declared a medieval 'forgery' seems not to have been aware of the possibility that the reason-ably-well-documented history of the Mandylion places it back in the third century, when it could very well have been stowed away during a flood for safe keeping and forgotten. It was rediscovered during the rebuilding of one of the ancient gates of Edessa in 525AD.

Be all this as it may, the authenticity of the Holy Shroud scarcely impinges on the Faith of Christians, since, as we have already noted, Faith is a gift of God and as such requires no support. There is no denying, though, that authenticating the Shroud would be of great comfort to many Christians.

The 'Development' of Doctrine

As our Catholic understanding grows, we realize that much of what we now accept to be undeniable is to be found only *seminally* in the New Testament. Here again we find hindsight to be a great help. The New Testament was written in the Jewish idiom mainly for Jews of the first and second centuries. The Church caters for the people of its own age. Our modern problems could hardly have been envisaged by those far-off people. They dealt with their own problems as well as they could, as succeeding generations discovered. (See 'Time-Conditioning', p. 51.)

That is how Doctrine began to develop. As the Church became more aware of its role in the world and of the changing needs of the people it was sent to serve, so its understanding of the truths with which it had been entrusted would grow at the same time.

The questions set out in the box opposite are some of the Questions that arise from statements found in the Bible. Whatever answers/solutions there are, they will have to have taken account of the mind-set – firstly, of those who made the initial statements; and secondly, the understanding of those to whom the statements were made.

What the Early Christians Wanted to Know

Just as their forbears had wanted an explanation of the beginnings of things, the early Christians will have wanted to know:- What parts of the Scriptures can we accept as the Word of God?[19] In what sense are we the 'adopted children of God'? Was Christ really talking to Nicodemus about Infant Baptism? Peter is the Rock on which the Church is built. . . but in what sense is he the Rock? What is meant by 'Grace'? Does the role of Mary, in the Birth of Jesus Christ, end in Bethlehem? If man is a 'sacrificing being', in what way is the Catholic Mass a Sacrifice? How can the Eucharist now be the Real Presence of Christ?

If you remember what has been said about Revelation,[20] you may understand how it has taken Mankind so many centuries to graduate from the use of 'myths' to the teachings of a recognizable Authority able to address such questions – and, with the passage of time, some of the answers need continual adjustment. As history teaches us, as ages come and go, the important questions get to be answered and to crop up again later; the others get put on the back-burner.

Dogmas

The definitive answers which the Church provides are offered to Catholics for their acceptance as true and are called Dogmas. When the time is considered to be 'right', such truths are defined by the Pope in a special ceremony in Rome attended by all the Bishops from across the world. It is worth pointing out that the Pope does not make a habit of doing this, not least because of the enormous costs involved. Such definitions take place perhaps once in a 100 years!

The Truths of the Apostles' Creed

The Apostles' Creed (p. 63) lists the Truths that Christians hold to be incontrovertible; not just that they exist, but that their existence is paramount, which is another way of saying of each, to misquote the 'Grand Inquisitor': 'of *each* there is no manner of doubt, no probable, possible, shadow of doubt, no possible doubt whatever!' (*The Gondoliers* Act 1: W.S. Gilbert).

Experience tells us that when **certainty** is found to be necessary, it will also be possible, and few would deny this necessity when it regards the significance of Man's knowledge of his destiny. Incidentally, those credal tenets do not comprise a list of Truths in descending order of priority. They are so interconnected that it is not possible to have one without the other. They are all, without exception, accepted as equals.

'I believe in. . . . **the Holy Catholic Church**' simply means that the Holy Catholic Church has all the means, not only to assist my presence in this world, but also to point out to me, now, the assurance of my eternal destiny; and of that there can be no question – just as there can be no question as to the existence of the Three Persons of God.

This is the simple basis for the doctrine of the **Indefectability** of the Church; which means that the Catholic Church can never collapse. The assurance that, in matters of Faith and Morals, the teachings of the Church (provided they *are* the teachings of the Church and not private opinions or misunderstood hearsay) cannot be in error, is also contained here.

The Pope leads the Catholic Church here in this world, his role being that of 'Shepherd and Teacher of all Christians'. When teaching on Faith and Morals for the observance of the whole world, he is *Infallible* – which means that not only is he protected from error (as we remember: Truth is not just the absence of error) but those pronouncements, described as infallible, possess 'something' of the Divine about them.

Henry VIII – 'Defender of the Faith'

King Henry VIII (of England) attempted, in 1521, to counter the teaching of his German contemporary, Luther, with a 'Dissertation on The Seven Sacraments' for which Pope Leo X gave him the title *Fidei Defensor* – 'Defender of the Faith' (*Fid Def.* or 'F.D.' appeared on all coinage displaying the monarch's head). By way of an aside, it has always been a curiosity among Catholics in England, that though the Constitution requires the Monarch to protect the Protestant religion (clearly from the effects of 'Rome'), it has never seen fit either to recognize it or repudiate its enjoyment of this singular Papal title.

What the Church taught on matters concerning 'Faith and Morals' and handed down from the Apostles through the Gospels, the Acts of the Apostles (and a later composite work known as 'Didache') to successive generations of Christians was called 'The Deposit of Faith'. However, even then, it was subject to misunderstanding and error.

Errors and Heresies

As early as the second century, as we have seen, there were individuals who queried Church doctrine

and proposed their own ideas. In successive generations Councils of Bishops met to discuss such
developments and it is against that background that
the Creeds were propounded. This is how 'heresy' (a
word describing a thesis that challenges a Dogma)
began to trouble the Church, with resulting measures,
some very harsh by modern standards, which were
invoked by the Church to protect the faithful from
false doctrine.

The Deposit of Faith was to be preached to the
World and protected against all who attacked it.
[There might not be much one could do about Sin as
we all share Man's sinful nature (p. 50). Sin appears,
on the surface, to be a private matter but Heresy was
of public concern and had to be rooted out.]

Since its earliest years the Catholic Church has had
to deal with such movements. As we have seen, the
Gospels were composed largely against a Jewish
background which their writers sought to convert. The
Old Testament reflects on the then contemporary
issues to remind its readers of God's Promises. In
much the same way, the Catholic Church is prompted
to teach wherever it finds error; it always refers to the
Sacred Scriptures (the Holy Bible) and to its traditions
when proclaiming a Truth. It usually does so only
when it recognizes a movement to deny it.

☐

The Reformation

Certainly, the moral directives of the Church have
been issued to correct an abuse of one or other of the
Commandments. It was the 'Deposit of Faith' that
Henry VIII sought to protect, and for that he received

his Papal entitlement of 'Defender of the Faith' (p. 105).

Apart from other issues, what prompted the Reformation in sixteenth century Europe was a misunderstanding regarding the nature of 'Punishment for Sin' as well as the 'means' necessary to avoid it. This went under the term 'Indulgences'; but with the abuses associated with these, together with an undeveloped theology of 'God's forgiveness' [you might remember 'time-conditioning' on p. 51], the Church at that time may have been insufficiently equipped to deal with it adequately.

The same may be said about the earlier cases of Copernicus and Galileo, whose scientific discoveries were thought to jeopardize the then Christian understanding of the nature of the cosmos. Apart from maths and physics (including the medicinal variety) all truth was then thought to be found within the pages of the Bible, and all problems to do with knowledge and behaviour were to be dealt with by recourse to the Bible or to the Church's teaching from which the Bible gained its authority.

Bible History

It is worth remembering that, had the Church not made it its own, the Bible would have remained, what it always had been, merely an extensive History of the religious development of the Hebrew Nation.

The Catholic Church must claim to contain the fullness of Christianity as it must to be loyal to the One who brought it into being from its 'Hebrew mother' – as may have become clear from what has already been discussed. The Church has used whatever means were at its disposal to protect the faithful from false notions, and its official pronouncements have been issued in every age[21] since the beginning of the Christian era. These are either the findings of the Councils of the Church, or Papal documents and Statements, dealing with localized disciplinary matters, and the more notable 'Encyclicals' that deal with universal matters of Faith or Morals.

As an institution the Catholic Church has been shown to be the world's foremost defender of 'human rights'. The Church clearly possesses the most sophisticated reasoning on all social matters. Its moral leadership, exercised without fear or favour, in a world that has become excessively liberal in its dealing with marginalized communities, can therefore scarcely be called in question.

What might be alarming to some is the Church's challenge to the way market economies are run and the suspect nature both of Capitalism and that of its recent predecessor, Communism. In a world which has gradually begun to shed its sense of responsibility, the Catholic Church as a community, with all its difficulties, has maintained its dependence on, and remained loyal to, the Christ who promised to be with it until the end of time (*Matthew* 28:20).

What is meant by 'Grace'?

Though this word has not been mentioned so far, it is important to consider it briefly. The word 'grace', taken from a Latin word for 'thanks', scarcely appears in the Old Testament. In the New Testament, where it appears frequently, it refers to 'God's favour', 'God's help', 'God's free gift'.

As Christian teaching developed, the word 'grace' was requisitioned to apply also to that 'gift' which was received first at Baptism and later referred to that divine assistance which is required by Man to persevere in doing good and avoiding evil. 'Grace' is taken to refer to the 'life' that the Christian receives from God through the Sacraments. 'Grace', therefore, belongs to the spiritual dimension of the human person that demands it for its continued dignified existence.

The Council of Carthage (N. Africa) in 417 first used this word in official Church teaching, which was repeated at the Second Council of Orange (France) in 529 and often enough afterwards, that God's Grace is needed in every human act, both for: 1) the perception and for the performance of what is right, and 2) that, without Grace, it is not possible to please God or to be 'saved'. Later Church teaching modified this last statement, but its general meaning has remained the same: namely that, though God destined Mankind, through Christ, to fulfil the Covenant promise made so long ago to Abraham, Man will require God's assistance to do so.

12 Priesthood & Laity

The building of Monasteries

THE POSSESSION of land has always meant power for its owner. In the fourteenth century BC, when the land of Canaan was being settled by the 12 Tribes of Israel, one of them, the Tribe of Levi, took no land but chose instead, as their 'portion', to minister to the people in all religious matters and undertake the priestly activity of 'sacrifice'. [One might therefore be cautious in criticising the Church for the power it exercises or for its wealth. Levi substituted this new position for its entitlement to land but in no sense did it lose its position among the 12 Tribes.]

After the cessation of (Levitical) priestly activity with the Destruction of the Temple in 70AD, Christians took over this priestly function. Eventually, the sacrificial nature of Christian worship evolved within the development of the 'Eucharist' (p. 86) and is now usually referred to as 'The Holy Mass'.

There was never a time in Catholic tradition where there has been no 'priesthood' or people to whom priests ministered. Hence the terms 'Priesthood & Laity'. Together they constitute the Church. [See pp. 114, 115.] When people speak of the 'Church' they tend to refer to the 'Clergy' (priests & deacons), or a Parish as 'belonging' to the priest. However, the Church is *all the people of God* with the 'parish community' belonging to its People.

Priestly Clothes

The panoply of ceremonial in the Catholic Church, so frowned on by the Reformers of sixteenth and seventeenth-century Europe, was but a continuation of Jewish traditions. The cut of the vestments used in Church services, which began during the fourth century, was largely dictated by Roman fashion. The oldest tradition for what Catholic clergy wore daily was the monastic habit which first appeared in the early Middle Ages. This was scarcely different from secular garb of the time; it was not as 'threatening' as the present 'dark suit and roman collar' (the 'dog collar') which became the norm around the mid-nineteenth century in England.

Now this is beginning to change back to an earlier practice (sixteenth century) when priests in normal clothes were indistinguishable from the Laity. The official Catholic directive requires clergy, when in public, to wear 'dark suits and roman collars'.

Whereas Western Christianity has tended to place its Clergy 'on a pedestal', the Eastern rites see them as part of the 'hoi polloi' – on a par with the people, and they are generally seen as separate only when presiding at the liturgical worship of the Church.

The Monasteries and Education

Fifth-century Europe saw the rise of Monasticism and the building of Monasteries. This was to cater for those who were looking for a way of life removed from what they considered to be a grossly unspiritual world; a world which betrayed itself in the pursuit of power by avarice and force of arms. As secularism overtook the principles of life laid down in the Gospels, the Catholic Church saw the need to recall mankind to its Christian roots. The monks then took on the work of preaching the Gospel in Europe and their role remains basically very much the same.

'Education' was left largely to the monks and their monasteries very soon became important seats of learning. The next 500 years saw the increase of religious orders of monks – and nuns too – whose life-style emphasized those aspects of Christianity which, until then, had been neglected. However, as the monasteries gained patronage, land and consequently power, abuses began to creep into their way of life yet again.

A reaction to this then produced the Mendicant Friars, the Franciscans, the Dominicans and Carmelites who gave up all their worldy possessions and ambitions. The numbers of monks and nuns grew to such an extent that a Christian became known either as a 'religious' or a 'lay person'. Later, as the temporal power of the Bishops increased[22] – with the acquiescence of the laity it must be added – though abuses continued to flourish, the respect given to the clergy was, generally speaking, 'ascribed' as opposed to 'acquired' as it still is today.

Structure of the Catholic Church

As noted earlier (pp. 23 & 26), no organization can hope to continue without considering its aims and how it will achieve them. For this there has to be Authority. Authority will: 1) Arise from within the group, where a member is elected to hold it. His authority is accepted by the group and the decisions are made, after consultation and with the agreement of the group – as in most democratic systems. 2) Arise from outside the group, when it is co-opted, delegated or deputized to fulfil some function. On being delegated, the group fulfils this function. There is normally no need for further consultation or recourse to this authority.

The Catholic Church sees itself as a divinely established family, and claims God's Authority to preach and to administer the Sacraments. This Authority, in so far as it is a Spiritual authority, is seen as coming from 'outside'; and is given to all equally in Baptism, so that the faithful can preach by example and administer the Sacraments of 'feeding' and 'forgiving'.

Authority also brings with it Power for its management. This authority arises from 'within' the group as the leaders are elected by the priests and people. It is here that difficulties arise. In the early Church, the administrative structures that developed were seen to have been imposed by God rather than, as is more probable, arising out of the day-to-day running of the

Church and coming from 'within'.

In such situations it is easy enough to confuse the two as in the case when one prays to God to be spared the loss of face and the legal punishment for some crime. The Scriptures give us a case in point. (Different sources usually have different agendas, hence one ought not to quote two different sources on one issue.) However, the Christ prays to be spared (*Matthew* 26:37-39) and yet, later, recognizes the authority of Pilate (*John* 19:10-11).

Administration of the Catholic Church

As Christianity moved away from the Jewish norms from which it developed it had to find its own leaders. In some places where synagogue officials became Christians, they continued to manage their communities as before. Those chosen for preaching however, now found they had no time to manage their communities as well as care for those in material need. So a new group (quite a departure from Jewish practice) of 'Servants' or 'Deacons' was established to care for the 'poor and the widows'. 'Bishops' (as shepherds) – presbyter bishops as they were called – were chosen to oversee/administer larger communities.

Jewish priests were to be found in the Temple before that was destroyed. But it would be yet a while before Christians found their own priests. Tradition says Peter, the one Christ appointed leader, went to Rome where he was betrayed and put to death c 67AD. The centre of Christianity moved to Rome after the fall of Jerusalem.

By the middle of the second century an adequate system of management had been established. The

Bishop of Rome, by then, was an accepted 'Successor' to the Apostle Peter, and was recognized as 'speaking with Peter's voice'. His role as Chief Shepherd became firmly established when the Emperor Constantine declared Christianity the state religion in place of paganism. In another 500 years the supremacy of Papal Authority, even over the Emperor was acknowledged. It was in Rome that Charlemagne was crowned Holy Roman Emperor on Christmas Day 800AD.

The Church Hierarchy

A list of the Bishops of Rome, the Popes, (some with chequered histories, some murdered, some elected by rival factions) is given at the end of this book. The Church spread, from these humble beginnings, through the work of the Missions as they understood the needs of individual communities; and it was from this initial system of 'Bishops', 'Priests' and 'Deacons' that the present hierarchy developed.

Clergy		Laity
Cardinals are drawn from all ranks of the clergy.	**Pope**	with the Clergy equally comprise the Church. The Clergy are commanded to feed God's people and are thus the servants of the Laity
	Archbishop	
Monsignor **Canon** **Dean**	**Bishop** Abbot/ Abbess **Priest**	
	Deacon	

Men, from the body of the Laity ask to be accepted for Ordination to the Permanent Diaconate or the Priesthood. It is from the local body of Priests that Deans are chosen to represent the Priests at the Bishop's Conference. Sometimes, the Dean is created 'Canon' to serve on the local Bishop's staff – known as the Chapter of Canons. Priests of special ability are created 'Monsignor' and given particular responsibility on the Bishop's staff. It is from the group of 'Monsignori' that Bishops are chosen.

The Bishop is in charge of a Collection of Parishes which is called a Diocese; also known as a See. [The Abbot, the senior monk in an Abbey/Monastery, has the rank of 'Monsignor' and sometimes the rank of Bishop.] Every Bishop, worldwide, is appointed by the Vatican in Rome after consultation with the Diocesan Staff concerned.

The senior Bishop in a Province or Diocese is an Archbishop. This is also a Vatican appointment. The senior Archbishop in a country is usually created a Cardinal. It is from the ranks of the Clergy that Cardinals are appointed by the Pope and it is from the College of Cardinals that the Pope is elected. From their number is chosen the Senate of the Supreme Pontiff to assist the Pope in the Government of the Church. They rank as Princes of royal blood, with the title of 'Eminence' and on the death of the Pope, they elect his successor from within their College. Cardinals are also appointed to Provinces as representatives of the Pope. They are members of the Diplomatic Corps and carry one of the following titles: 'Papal Legate', Papal Nuncio', 'Apostolic Delegate', depending on the diplomatic status that particular country enjoys with the Vatican.

13 Liturgy & Sacred Texts

Ornamental initial letter from a medieval Psalter

JERUSALEM in the tenth century BC saw the building of the first Temple which became the sole site for Hebrew sacrificial worship. All Temple rites and practices took place there in accordance with strict prescriptions laid down (*Book of Numbers* and *Leviticus*) to cater for the needs of the people and their time-honoured traditions.

Much Hebrew tradition was eventually taken over into Christian practice, with Jerusalem continuing for a while to be the headquarters of the early Church. However, within 30 years of Christ's Resurrection, this moved to Rome, the centre of the Empire, from where the developing Christian Missions were managed.

By AD 360 Christianity, under Constantine's imperial patronage, had become the 'established' religion to replace paganism. In this way Rome took on an importance for Christians that was not dissimilar to the position that Jerusalem held for Jews for more than a thousand years before Christ.

From the fourth century AD churches began to spring up all over Europe, with their Bishops being appointed from Rome and the manner of their worship according with developing Roman prescriptions. As the Church found itself entering areas of established pagan culture, some pagan festivals were taken over and 'Christianized', like our present 'Christmas'. This is only repeating the Hebrew requisitioning of Canaanite pastoral festivals (pp. 21, 86) over 1000 years before.

It is of considerable interest, though it is seldom remarked upon, that the major part of Catholic Liturgy, the readings during Catholic worship in church, is taken piecemeal from the Hebrew Scriptures. The manner of ritual, with the use of Vestments, Candles and Incense, is merely a development of what the early Church had made of Jewish traditions.

What *did* cause a stir, however, as we have seen (p. 98) was the emergence of Crucifixes (the figure of Christ on the Cross) and statues representing the Virgin Mary, Joseph, Angels and Saints. Seen as Idols, they were considered to contravene the first Commandment. They were in fact used as 'visual aids' for the instruction of Catechumens (those wishing to join the Church) and to assist the devotion of the faithful. Unfortunately, they also began to be given a special honour which tended to lead to superstition – and that was forbidden! In the main, provided such religious objects remained merely to remind the faithful of the truths of the Faith, they were permitted.

□

'Symbols' & 'Sight'

Symbols had been employed in the Rituals of the Old Testament to represent God's Covenant with the Patriarchs (p. 87) right up to Christ's time, and as these were naturally taken over into Christian usage as part of the Christian's Jewish heritage, their continued use in New Testament times would hardly have warranted special mention by Biblical writers.

Our ability to see things clearly depends largely on the available light; and the way we get to understand how things develop, more often than not, is achieved by hindsight (p. 13). The writers of the Old Testament lived in primitive times when the people had only a very short-term outlook on the future. They would not have had much idea of what the word 'future' meant. Today, having extensive and well classified historical information with which to feed our imaginations, we are in a much better position to make intelligent long-distance forecasts into the future.

This works both ways; working backwards, we can accurately trace the development of Old Testament thinking about the Promises which were continually being repeated through the Patriarchs and the Prophets up to the time of Christ. We read first of Man's primitive efforts to harness the powers of the seasons and bend them to his will (p. 14). This changes after he becomes aware of the existence of his God (p. 17).

The Old Testament shows signs of God's providence working in every generation; each one in turn being reminded of God's Promise (p. 29). The gradual awareness of the spiritual nature of this intercourse will take some 2,000 years to emerge, so that by the time the Christ arrives, Mankind is capable of receiving some understanding of the Promise, now about to be fulfilled.

For the author of *John's Gospel*, the Promise is fulfilled at the moment of Christ's appearing! Man's awareness of this fact, however, like before, continues to be a gradual process for every succeeding generation. Time-conditioning, as in the Old Testament, will demand that its expression will change with the passage of time. The way geological phenomena like stalagmites and stalactites are still being formed after millions of years, will give some idea of the length of time it might take visibly to establish a universal spiritual 'network' that can call itself the Family of God.

We know that the appearance of the Christ was an historic moment. But the transition from Old Testament thinking (with its emphasis on Jewish traditions and the Law) to New Testament life, with its Christian overtones, took some time. The Old Testament symbols were gradually transformed into 'signs' that would recall, not so much God's Promise but would intensify Man's awareness of Christ's enduring Presence in the New.

As this transformation gathered momentum in the Church, Catholics began to call it the *Sacramental*

System. This transformation is a continuing phenomenon, and, as has been said already, it is always 'in the process of beginning'. All that has been said in this section is 'made real' through the **Seven Sacraments of the Church**.

One important question for the earliest Christians was: What did Christ mean by his command at the Last Supper: 'Do this in my Memory'? The ceremony called the 'Breaking of Bread', after the initiating practice of Baptism, was *the* celebration which drew together the emerging community of those Jews who believed in Jesus. Special Jewish religious celebrations were performed to recall the past in such a way as 'to make some past event present again' (pp. 87, 89).

For Christians the 'Breaking of Bread' recalled the Last Supper and Christ's presence at it. It somehow made present again the Risen Christ who, now risen from the dead, was hidden from their eyes. It was in the 'Breaking of Bread' that the Risen Lord was seen to be present among the assembled community. But how did the early Christians, especially those without a Jewish background, understand the relationship between the 'Breaking of Bread' (called the 'Eucharist') and the Real Presence of the Risen Lord? Searching for an appropriate term they chose a Latin word: 'Sacramentum' meaning 'a sign that contained/produced what it signified'. 'Sacramentum' translated a Greek word for something 'hidden/mysterious', and 'sign /symbol' and was first used by Tertullian (†225) in referring to the vow Christians take at Baptism.

As the secret enshrined in Baptism could be called a 'Sacrament' ('a sacred sign that gives grace') it seemed appropriate that the Eucharist also be described as a Sacrament. This sort of language took generations to develop principally because it had no specific precedent in the language of the Old Testament;[23] and it was on this language that the early Church was almost totally dependent. Much Catholic doctrine centres around the word 'Sacrament'.

The Seven Sacraments

The Promise made in the Old Testament is conveyed at the initiation ceremony: **Baptism** (Christening). Communal recognition of our sharing in its understanding (as far as humanly possible) is fed through the **Eucharist**. An adult commitment to this understanding is strengthened by the Bishop in the **Confirmation** ceremony. Inability and weakness are both taken care of in the Sacrament of **Reconciliation**, which brings with it an encouragement that needs to be shared with others and is reflected in the Lord's Prayer in which Forgiveness is sought. While these four Sacraments are established for the general needs of the Church, they are open to all, once the initiation has taken place.

The final three are for the specific needs of the local community: the **Sacrament of the Sick** brings both spiritual and physical healing to those who are indisposed, either to the individual or to a group. **Marriage** unites Man and Woman within the local neighbourhood to assist them in their life together and for the growth and nurture of their community – it is here that families are joined together. The spiritual needs of the local community are met by the Bishop when, having chosen whom he sees fit for this particular Ministry, solemnly commissions him in the **Sacrament of Holy Orders**.

'While such a system, rooted in the past, must obviously have been highly beneficial during those ages when there were no other agencies to assist and strengthen communities in which they clearly played an important part, living in a brave new modern world, one has to move forward and that cannot be done with such out-dated systems, no matter how good they were. You only have to look at what has happened to *Marriage*!'   *Good point!*

By way of an answer: If it be true that fewer Christian people are getting married – whatever reasons they may have for putting it off – it would show that Marriage values still count for something – and that such folk, then, may feel incapable of making the requisite commitment. You would have to change the *make-up of the human person* before: (1) 'love' (p. 65) which happens to be the strongest of desires between the sexes, could be obliterated; and before: (2) the personal rights and obligations/ privileges that belong to the partners in Marriage cease to exist.

Were either of these to be found hypothetically possible, on present counting it would take another 5,000 years to develop from now; and, of course, since we can only speak from experience, it would have to start from an equally primitive mind-set from which our present system has developed. Without wishing to offend, this cannot be saying much for the mind-set of those who wish to change the present system, or who complain about their Marriages, or the Church's teaching on Marriage.

The brave new world would not be able to move any distance without recognizing its debt to the initial, primitive, and later faltering steps of our ancestors.

Like them, we need an agreed understanding of Marriage, and if there is to be any hope of success we need to go back to the garage wall and see what the Manufacturer's Guide book has to say (p. 83).

'Christ's Role in the World'

By way of another detour, it is understood that, for some, the Bible contains the Sole Rule of Faith and Behaviour for everyone of every time and place (pp. 96, 102). We now know that those who compiled the Old Testament had no idea *how or when* their prophecies were to be fulfilled; or that the people responsible for the composition of the New Testament foresaw all the difficulties that would be faced in future generations.

It would be injudicious, therefore, to suggest that the Biblical writers might have cut-and-dried answers to the political and economic problems besides the religious ones, that might be experienced 2,000 years in the future.

It would help to remember that the purpose of *John's Gospel* was to demonstrate Christ's role in the world as it was *then*, so obviously *'there were many other things that Jesus did and said that are not written in this book'* (*John* 20:30 & 21:25). That writer was aware of the problems facing his community as a result of what Christ had done and what he had said. He knew of the existence of other contemporary traditions but chose not to include them in his Gospel because they did not serve his purpose.

If we recall that the material in the New Testament reflects the needs of its time (first and second centuries AD), and how often it is difficult to associate some of these needs with Christ's reported words, we may get the flavour of the difficulties that beset later generations who met other difficulties as they come to grips with the phenomenon of Christ foreseen in the Old Testament and charted in the New Testament. It is with this in mind that we look to that Authority which gave the Hebrew Scriptures to the world and declared them to be God's Words a short 2,000 years ago.

The Catholic Position on Life & Death

WE come now to the most important TEACHING of all, important because it actually affects us deeply; and how it is that we fit in with something that has been discussed before.

Having dealt fairly quickly with the 'Me', (p. 24) and, now that I am here, how I must treat others as I treat 'Myself', I find that what I want most in life is 'happiness', so it will not be strange to suggest that I want it 'never to end'. This is a fact of life; and whatever word I prefer to use instead of *'happiness'* – the 'endlessness' of it is essential to my wanting it. . . and wanting it *now!*

The rejoinder to that statement usually is: 'But everyone has got to die!' To which the quiet reply is: We are talking about 'what we want' – so we are not talking about death, which, right now, is presumably 'what we *do not* want'! For the majority of people the world over, death is not an escape, but for many with a superstitious frame of mind, 'death is the end!'

The Catholic position is quite the reverse. Since it is natural for Man to want 'not to die' (that idea is to be found, once again, in *Genesis* and is referred to by St

Paul),[24] we might begin to see a deeper meaning in the Promise made by God to Abraham. Hindsight again tells us, and from reason alone, that it is odd that Abraham should have been promised by God that he would become a great nation. . . and then, aged 175, die! Evil/Sin and Death, of which we are all aware, come into this story together.

Christianity teaches that Christ fulfils the Promise God made to Abraham, by putting an end to these two impostors, Sin and Death, that are arguably Man's ultimate enemies. By his *Rising from the Dead*, the God-Man, Christ Jesus, has demonstrated this for all time. In accepting this we begin to see a purpose, not only behind the Creation story in *Genesis*, but also behind the gradual unfolding of the often-repeated Promise to Abraham. Then come the difficulties experienced by the initially superstitious Hebrews, even when assisted by their Prophets, and then, moving into the Christian era, the developments made by successive generations to keep this Promise in the minds of the faithful.

Thus, rather than death being the end, in the Catholic mind-set, death is really only the beginning – the beginning of something new, just as Christ's Resurrection is something new, a 'newness' that we celebrate during the Holy Mass. The whole of the New Testament points to this: in particular the writings of St John, who associates Man's destiny with that of the Christ. There is extensive coverage of this in the *Letter to the Romans*.[25]

Is There Another Name for God?

Is there another name for God besides 'God'? It seems that every religious tradition has a list of different names. Of course, the more gods, the more names. In the beginning of their history the Hebrews used pagan names for God – they were the only ones to hand! They learnt that God's proper name (*Exodus* Ch. 3) to be **Jahweh**, or **Jehovah** (same consonants, different vowels). It was later held to be so sacred, that speaking it was forbidden because of the First Commandment. But before the 12th cent BC, **Adonai, Elohim, El Shaddai, El Elyon, Roi, El Berith, El Olam**, titles of local gods, were extracted from Canaanite life and there is no reason for denying their being assimilated into Hebrewism. However, only the first three appear in the modern Bible.

14 Pilgrimages & Holy Places

Canterbury Cathedral, Kent

Holy Places

THE MIDDLE EAST in the seventh century AD saw the rise of Islam. Another Semitic religion, it was looked on by 'outsiders' in the same way as the Romans saw Christianity – as a quasi-political movement with religious overtones.

Quickly spreading through Asia Minor into the West, Islam took Jerusalem from the Jews and the Christians. The Crusades, starting in the eleventh century, were European attempts to recapture

Jerusalem from these 'Moors' and eclipsed much Christian missionary thinking during the Middle Ages.

Jerusalem had been a place of pilgrimage for Jews from the tenth century BC. It would take a further 2000 years before it could be *settled* as a divided city with its Jewish, Christian and Muslim quarters. The Mosque known as the Dome of the Rock occupies the site of the ancient Jewish Temple and dominates the skyline.

Rome, of course, with its Colosseum, the site of much suffering during the persecution of the Christians, had become the seat of Christendom, the Chair of the Supreme Pontiff, the chief Bishop of the Holy Catholic Church. The Basilica of St Peter, as it was believed to be the site of the Tomb of St Peter, the leader of the Apostles, was the place of pilgrimage.

The most notable place of pilgrimage in England is the Cathedral at **Canterbury** where, in 1170, Archbishop Thomas à Becket was murdered on the 'orders' of King Henry II. Chaucer's *Canterbury Tales* gives an idea of the way pilgrimages were conducted in the Middle Ages.

Down the centuries the Church has made much of the Virgin Mary, as she had a special share in the Coming of the Christ. As we celebrate Christ as the 'King of Kings' it is only proper that Mary should be honoured as the 'Queen Mother'. The most notable shrines built in her honour in Europe are at **Aylesford** and **Walsingham** (in England), **Knock** (Ireland), **Czestochowa** (Poland), **Fatima** (Portugal), **Lourdes** (S.France), with **Guadalupe** (in Mexico). **Croagh Patrick** (Ireland) is a place of pilgrimage where St Patrick is honoured.

The Grotto of Massabielle, Lourdes

Monte Cassino in northern Italy is the site of the famous Benedictine Monastery which was destroyed during World War II. It is a place of pilgrimage as were many Abbeys in England during the Middle Ages. One reason for this was the saintly monks, considered to have a 'hot line' to God, who were able to encourage the faithful in their pursuit of holiness.

The Abbeys in England, sadly, were dissolved by Henry VIII in 1539. Abbey lands and property were given to the Lords and Barons thus tying them more tightly to the Throne. In mainland Europe Church lands and privileges faired more favourably during the Reformation. The Church in Germany would have to wait for the rigourous Secularization of its Monasteries and properties that took place at the beginning of the nineteenth century.

However, the history of the Church's development from the fifth century, with the increase of its temporal power, demands a more formalized study than one might expect from this simple volume.

The city of London in the Middle Ages had a church every 100 yards! Each had its coterie of Clergy, Altar 'staff' and Choir but even then not everyone attended Mass on Sundays and other Holy Days.

To return to simple matters, which is where we began, the normal place of worship throughout Christendom is the village church around which all the people's dwellings are built, and is the spiritual and temporal centre of life in all rural areas. It has been so in England since the Faith was first brought here in the time of Julius Caesar. Christianity spread first from Jerusalem, and later from Rome, throughout what came to be known as 'Christendom', under the influence of the Missionary Monks during the following centuries.

'The Faith Journey' Revisited

Our journey through this book began with a scene in the Basilica of the Holy Sepulchre. From this Basilica it is 400 yards to the Dome of the Rock, sacred to the Muslim culture. This Rock in turn stands on the foundations of the Jewish Temple, taking us back to 1000BC, the ancient stones of which presently comprise the Wailing Wall.

In much the same way as the *Acts of the Apostles* (the last historical Book in the New Testament) begins in Jerusalem and ends in Rome, that is what we have done in a rather round-about way. As the adage says: '*All roads lead to Rome*'. As in all journeys, one stops off occasionally to look at points of interest, even taking several looks; but there are plenty more of those that we have not touched.

The Faith Journey that was mentioned earlier is of universal concern, and while everyone is involved, it is not always possible or even convenient to take note of all that happens on the trip. Since we joined it relatively recently, it is good to remember that it has been going a very long time! It is not yet 1m days since Christ walked in this world – yet it has been suggested that Man has been around for over 30m years! So while Christianity is still in its 'early days', hindsight is very useful in learning how it is possible for the Catholic Church to get as far as it has.

Further exploration, then, is recommended, and since it is easily available, why not take the opportunity to do so? Make sure, though, that the light is right (p. 13) – you cannot see much in the dark.[26] It is only a suggestion, but your best bet would be to engage an authorized guide who knows the country, even some useful short cuts, and who has both the knowledge and the authority to explain things a bit better.

E.H.

Bibliography

Guide to the Holy Land by Eugene Hoade OFM: Franciscan Press, Jerusalem 1981

The Jerusalem Bible: Darton, Longman & Todd 1974

The Jerome Biblical Commentary: Geoffrey Chapman 1980

Documents of the Christian Church: Henry Bettenson World's Classics 1959

Enchiridion Symbolorum: Herder 1957

On Genesis: by Bruce Vawter: Geoffrey Chapman 1977

Theology for the Third Millennium: H. Kung: Harper Collins 1988

Further Reading

Your Faith, *A Popular Presentation of Catholic Belief*, Redemptorist Publications, Hampshire 1996

Biblical Exegesis & Church Doctrine by R.E. Brown, London 1985

Official Catholic Teachings: Bible Interpretation ed. by J.J. Megiven (Consortium Book; Wilmington, NC: McGrath, 1978)

The Teaching of the Catholic Church by Herbert McCabe OP, CTS London 1985

The Documents of Vatican II ed. by W.M. Abbott and J. Gallagher

Focus on Faith, *A Resource for the Journey into the Catholic Church* by Deborah M. Jones: Suffolk 1996

Faith Alive ed. Rowan Pascoe & J. Redford: London 1994

Understanding Catholicism by Monika Hellwig, Ramsey, NJ 1981

Mere Christianity, *The Case for Christianity, Christian Behaviour and beyond Personality* by C.S. Lewis: London 1952

The Problem of Pain by C.S. Lewis: Harper Collins, London 1977

Catholic Faith by Roderick Strange: Oxford 1986

Catholicism by Richard McBrien: London 1994

Catechism of the Catholic Church: London 1994

Notes

1. (p. 11) Theology was clearly the highest of man's pursuits. In worldly affairs the Popes exercised their traditional primacy of jurisdiction over the universal Church. No one was his senior! So 'when the Pope spoke, that was the end of the matter'.

2. (p. 15) The historical dating of the Hebrew story, throughout this book, is taken from archaeological and non-biblical information as it becomes available to us.

3. (p. 29) see page 104 on the unchangeable nature of the Church's mission.

4. (p. 32) The Hebrew attitude to 'history' has been referred to (p. 15).

5. (p. 36) The Hebrews, unlike the Egyptians, were not in the habit of leaving detailed inscriptions on walls or pottery. For dates like these we have to rely on Egyptian hieroglyphs & archaeological sources.

6. (p. 40) All quotations from the Bible, or citations to which you might refer, are to be found in that version known as the *Jerusalem Bible* (Darton, Longman & Todd) first published in 1974

7. (p. 43) Plenty of instances in the New Testament refer to what was thought of Christ: Mt.14:1-2, Mk.6:14-16, Lk.9:7-9, Mt.16:13-20, Mk.8:27-30, Lk.9:18-21

8. (p. 45) This truth is stated categorically in John's First Letter 3:1

9. (p. 48) Copernicus *thought* that the Earth moved round the Sun. Rome put his book on the Index (of forbidden books). When Galileo published this as a *fact* in the face Rome's then somewhat fundamentalist approach to Scripture, he was in trouble – being forced, in 1633, to abjure his findings by the Roman Inquisition!

10. (p. 50) This subject is dealt with extensively in St Paul's Letter to the Romans. This quotation is found in Chap. 5:12

11. (p. 50) St John's Gospel 1:29 . . .*'that takes away the sin of the world.'* are found in the Authorized and Revised Standard versions. The Latin Vulgate, Jerusalem Bible, and

some other versions, omit these words. Even so, the tenor of John's Gospel, the end of Luke's and the rest of Paul's Romans Chap. 5 especially v 17: . . .*Jesus Christ will cause everyone who recieved the free gift that he does not deserve, of being made 'righteous'* all give a clue as to how the Scriptures indicate God's intention regarding Sin!

12. (p. 51) Romans 6:23

13. (p. 65) Jn.1:29. See footnote below.

14. (p. 66) Jn.15:13. When citing the Scriptures one has always to take into account the context in which they are found; and guard against a tendency to make use of such quotations to justify a position that, in fact, is not necessarily in the mind of the writer being quoted.

15. (p. 69) The point concerning the importance of the 'Me' was made on page 24

16. (p. 80) Mk 12:29ff gives Christ's answer during a debate on this subject.

17. (p. 87) How much 'later' cannot be gauged scientifically. Abraham's story, since it used to be attributed to Moses (until the 1930s), was dated some 650 years after that event. It is now accepted that the Pentateuch (the first five books of the Old Testament) was put together during the period of the Kings some 200 years after Moses. So to *date* this 'later thinking' we could be speaking of about *500 years* later!

18. (p. 92) The presently-named Greek Orthodox Church has a different day for Easter, usually about a fortnight later. The argument over which Day on which to hold Easter was one cause for that part of the Catholic Church which, in 1054, 'split away' and refused to accept the authority vested in the Bishop of Rome, the Pope. Because of this split, some think that 1054 marked the beginning of the Roman Catholic Church. However, since the Greek refusal to accept its authority, the Catholic Church can easily be verified historically: it must have been in existence for the Greeks to split away from it.

19. (p. 103) 'I would not believe the Gospel did not have the authority of the Catholic Church to move me to this' St Augustine: *An Answer to The Manichaean Letter* 5.6 (c 397AD). But it was at the Council of Trent (1546), after centuries of hesitation, that the 'Canon' of the Scriptures was firmly and

finally fixed for the whole of Christendom.

20. (p. 103) 'God's revelation can only be perceived through human experience which is why it takes so long for it to be understood as such.'

21. (p. 108) 'Documents of the Christian Church' Oxford University Press

22. (p. 112) By the ninth century it was recognized that the head of the Holy Roman Empire held his Imperial title from the Pope. Since the eighth century it was accepted that Constantine had decreed a gift of the islands of the West to the Papacy (fifteenth-century examination proved this a forgery and it is now discredited and the Pope-Emperor relationship gradually reversed). To give an idea of Papal power in those days one example will suffice: Hadrian VI (1154-59) the only English Pope, bestowed the lordship of Ireland on the English king Henry II.

23. (p. 122) cf also page 87 where the blood of the animal was used as a symbol of the Covenant with Moses.

24. (p. 125) Gen. 2:17, 3:4: the 2nd half of St Paul's Letter to the Romans: in particular 5:12

25. (p. 126) St Paul's Letter to the Romans 6:5

26. (p. 132) *A man can walk in the daytime without stumbling because he has the light of this world to see by; but if he walks at night he stumbles because there is no light to guide him* (Gospel according to John 11:9–10)

List of Popes

Name	Year	Name	Year	Name	Year
Peter	48	Zosimus	417	John V	685
Linus	69	Boniface I	418	Conon	686
Cletus	78	*Eulalius**	*418*	*Theodore**	*687*
Clement I	90	Celestine I	422	*Paschal**	*687*
Evaristus	99	Sixtus III	432	Sergius I	687
Alexander I	105	Leo I	440	John VI	701
Sixtus I	115	Hilarius	461	John VII	705
Telesphorus	125	Simplicius	468	Sisinnius	708
Hyginus	136	Felix II	483	Constantine I	708
Pius I	140	Gelasius I	492	Gregory II	715
Anicetus	155	Anastasius II	496	Gregory III	731
Soter	166	Symmachus	498	Zachary	741
Eleutherus	175	*Laurentius**	*498*	Stephen II	752
Victor I	189	Hormisdas	514	Stephen III	752
Zephyrinus	199	John I	523	Paul I	757
Calistus I	217	Felix III	526	*Constantine II†*	*767*
*Hippolytus**	*217*	Boniface II	530	*Philip**	*768*
Urban I	222	*Dioscorus**	*530*	Stephen IV	768
Pontianus	230	John II	533	Hadrian I	772
Anterus	235	Agapitus I	535	Leo III	795
Fabian	236	*Silverius**	*536*	Stephen V	816
Cornelius	251	Vigilius	537	Paschal I	817
Novatian	*251*	Pelagius I	556	Eugenius II	814
Lucius I	253	John III	551	Valentine	827
Stephen I	254	Benedict I	575	Gregory IV	827
Sixtus II	257	Pelagius II	579	Sergius II	844
Dionysius	259	Gregory I	590	*John**	*844*
Felix I	269	Sabinianus	604	Leo IV	847
Eutychianus	275	Boniface III	607	Benedict III	855
Caius	283	Boniface IV	608	*Anastasius**	*855*
Marcellinus	296	Adeodatus I	615	Nicholas I	858
Marcellus I	308	Boniface V	619	Hadrian II	867
Eusebius	309	Honorius I	625	John VIII	872
Militades	311	Severinus	640	Marinus I	882
Sylvester I	314	John IV	640	Hadrian III	884
Mark	336	Theodore I	642	Stephen VI	885
Julius I	337	Martin I*	649	Formosus	891
Liberius	352	Eugenius I	654	Boniface VI	896
*Felix II**	*355*	Vitalian	657	Stephen VII†	896
Damasus I	366	Adeodatus II	672	Romanus	897
*Ursinus**	*366*	Donus	676	Theodore II	897
Siricius	384	Agatho	678	John IX	898
Anastasius I	399	Leo II	682	Benedict IV	900
Innocent I	401	Benedict II	684	Leo V†	903

Christopher†	903	Nicholas II	1059	Nicholas III	1277
Sergius III	904	Alexander II	1061	Martin IV	1281
Anastasius III	911	*Honorius II**	*1061*	Honorius IV	1285
Lando	913	Gregory VII	1073	Nicholas IV	1288
John X†	914	*Clement III**	*1080*	Celestine V*	1294
Leo VI†	928	Victor III	1086	Boniface VIII	1294
Stephen VIII†	928	Urban II	1088	Benedict XI	1303
John XI*	931	Paschal II	1099	Clement V	1305
Leo VII	936	*Theodoric**	*1100*	John XXII	1316
Stephen IX	939	*Albert**	*1102*	*Nicholas V**	1328
Marinus II	942	*Sylvester IV*	*1105*	Benedict XII	1334
Agapitus II	946	Gelasius II	1118	Clement VI	1342
John XII*	955	*Gregory VIII**	*1118*	Innocent VI	1352
Leo VIII*	963	Callistus II	1119	Urban V	1362
Benedict V*	964	Honorius II	1124	Gregory XI	1370
Leo VIII (again)	964	*Celestine**	*1124*	Urban VI	1378
John XIII	965	Innocent II	1130	Boniface IX	1389
Benedict VI†	973	*Analetus II*	*1130*	Innocent VII	1404
*Boniface VII**	974	*Victor IV**	*1138*	Gregory XII*	1406
Benedict VII	974	Celestine II	1143	*Clement VII*	*1378*
John XIV†	983	Lucius II†	1144	*Benedict XIII**	*1394*
Boniface VII (again)†		Eugenius III	1145	*Clement VIII**	*1423*
	984	Anastasius IV	1153	Alexander V	1409
John XV	985	Hadrian IV	1154	*John XXIII**	*1410*
Gregory V	996	Alexander III	1159	Martin V	1417
*John XVI**	997	*Victor IV*	*1159*	Eugenius IV	1431
Sylvester II	999	*Paschal III*	1164	*Felix V**	*1439*
John XVII	1003	*Callistus III**	1168	Nicholas V	1447
John XVIII	1004	*Innocent III**	1179	Callistus III	1455
Sergius IV	1009	Lucius III	1181	Pius II	1458
Benedict VIII	1012	Urban III	1185	Paul II	1464
*Gregor**	*1012*	Gregory VIII	1187	Sixtus IV	1471
John XIX	1024	Clement III	1187	Innocent VIII	1484
Benedict IX*	1032	Celestine III	1191	Alexander VI	1492
Sylvester III*	1045	Innocent III	1198	Pius III	1503
Benedict IX (again)		Honorius III	1216	Julius II	1503
	1045	Gregory IX	1227	Leo X	1513
Gregory VI*	1045	Celestine IV	1241	Hadrian VI	1522
Clement II	1046	Innocent IV	1243	Clement VII	1523
Benedict IX (again)		Alexander IV	1254	Paul III	1534
	1047	Urban IV	1261	Julius III	1550
Damasus II	1048	Clement IV	1265	Marcellus II	1555
Leo IX	1049	Gregory X	1271	Paul IV	1555
Victor II	1055	Innocent V	1276	Pius IV	1559
Stephen X	1057	Hadrian V	1276	Pius V	1566
*Benedict X**	*1058*	John XXI	1276	Gregory XIII	1572

Sixtus V	1585	Innocent XI	1676	Pius VIII	1829
Urban VII	1590	Alexander VIII	1689	Gregory XVI	1831
Gregory XIV	1590	Innocent XII	1691	Pius IX	1846
Innocent IX	1591	Clement XI	1700	Leo XIII	1878
Clement VIII	1592	Innocent XIII	1721	Pius X	1903
Leo XI	1605	Benedict XIII	1724	Benedict XV	1914
Paul V	1605	Clement XII	1730	Pius XI	1922
Gregory XV	1621	Benedict XIV	1740	Pius XII	1939
Urban VIII	1623	Clement XIII	1758	John XXIII	1958
Innocent X	1644	Clement XIV	1769	Paul VI	1963
Alexander VII	1655	Pius VI	1775	John Paul I	1978
Clement IX	1667	Pius VII	1800	John Paul II	1978
Clement X	1670	Leo XII	1823		

Dates pre-175 are conjectural. Those in *italics* ('Antipopes') elected unlawfully by splinter groups, and not counted among the 263 to date.
Those * abdicated, resigned or deposed.
Those † met violent deaths other than martyrdom.
There was no Pope John XX
Pope John XXI was killed in a building accident.

Catholics/Christians Worldwide

According to the 1994 Roman Almanac, the Roman Catholic Church worldwide totals 937m. This does not account for the members of Uniate Churches of the Middle East in union with Rome. There are other Christian groups not in union with Rome, namely the Greek Orthodox and Russian Orthodox Churches and also the various Protestant Churches.

While the total number of Christians may be considerable, out of an estimated world population of 5bn, the Roman Catholic Church holds a membership of around 17%.

Books of the Bible listed by Catholic Church

OLD TESTAMENT

THE PENTATEUCH (completed c 10th C. BC)
The Book of Genesis
The Book of Exodus
The Book of Leviticus
The Book of Numbers
The Book of Deuteronomy (with later adjustments)

THE HISTORICAL BOOKS
The Book of Joshua (still being reworked in 6th C. BC)
The Book of Judges (1st edition at end of 8th C. BC)
The Book of Ruth (10th C. BC)
The First Book of Samuel (6th C. BC)
The Second Book of Samuel (separated in 2nd C. BC)
The First Book of Kings (c550BC)
The Second Book of Kings (c550BC)

THE WISDOM BOOKS
The Book of Job (between 600-450BC)
The Book of Psalms (finalized c386AD)
The Book of Proverbs (8th C. BC with later additions)

THE PROPHETS
Isaiah (3 separate Books: between c783-c510BC)
Jeremiah (627-598BC)

The Books of Ezra and Nehemiah (c400BC)
The First Book of Chronicles (completed c300BC)
The Second Book of Chronicles (completed c300BC)
The Book of Tobit (c200BC but not in Hebrew Bible)
The Book of Judith (c150BC)
The Book of Esther (completed by 114BC)
The First Book of Maccabees (completed by 63BC)
The Second Book of Maccabees (completed by 63BC)

The Book of Ecclesiastes (4th or 3rd C. BC)
The Song of Songs (a collection: trad. 10th C. BC)
The Book of Wisdom (c150BC)
The Book of Ecclesiasticus (c180BC)

Amos (c760BC)
Obadiah (mid 5th C. BC)
Jonah (between 400-200BC)

Lamentations (beginning of 6th C. BC)
Baruch (between 597-538BC)
Ezekiel (c593-568BC)
Daniel (c165BC)
Hosea (between 750-732 BC)
Joel (c400BC)

Micah (between 742-687BC)
Nahum (c651BC)
Habakkuk (between 605-597BC: after Nahum)
Zephaniah (c640-609BC)
Haggai (c520BC)
Zechariah (c520-517BC)
Malachi (mid 5th C. BC)

NEW TESTAMENT

The GOSPELS according to:
Matthew (shortly? after 70AD)
Mark (65-70AD)

Luke (between 70-85?AD)
John (c90-100AD)
Acts of the Apostles (between 80-85?AD)

St PAUL'S LETTERS to:
the Romans (late 57-early 58AD)
The First to the Corinthians (early 57AD)
The Second to the Corinthians (late 57AD)
the Galatians (54-55AD)
the Ephesians (after 63AD)
the Philippians (61-63AD)
the Colossians (between 61-63AD)

The First to the Thessalonians (51AD)
The Second to the Thessalonians (a few months later)
The First to Timothy (between 66-67AD)
The Second to Timothy (c67AD)
Titus (c65AD)
Philemon (between 61-63AD)
the Hebrews (after 70AD)

The Letter of St James (before 62AD)
St Peter's First Letter (c64AD)
St Peter's Second Letter (c64AD)
St John's First Letter (end of 1st C. AD)

St John's Second Letter (end of 1st C. AD)
St John's Third Letter (end of 1st C. AD)
St Jude's Letter (c90AD)
The Book of Revelation (between 90-96AD)
also known as The Apocalypse

Index

Abraham 15, 29, 30, 53, 87, 91, 109, 126
Alexander the Great 30, 31
Alexandria 31, 62
Anabaptists 28
Anaximanda 10
Apostle's Creed 62, 63, 93, 97, 104
Apostles 62
Aquinas, Thomas 75
Archaeology 17
Aristotle 10, 18, 75
Arius, Arian 62
Assumption 92
Aylesford shrine 129

Baal 21
Baptism 23, 24, 62, 63, 103, 113, 121, 122
Bar Mitzvah 23
Becket, Thomas 129
Benediction 93
Berengarius 93
Bible 15
Bishops 62, 103, 106, 112, 114, 115, 116, 118
Bolt, Robert 28
Byzantium 101

Calvary, Mount 94
Canaanites, Canaan 21, 22, 65, 71, 86, 110, 118
Canterbury 129
Cardinal 115, 116
Carmelite Friars 112
Carthage, Council of 109
Charlemagne 115
Christ/Jesus 25, 26, 27, 31, 34, 35-37, 39, 41, 43, 44, 50, 52, 53, 55, 61, 62, 65, 66, 79, 88-92, 94, 95, 97, 98, 99, 101, 103, 120, 121, 124, 126

Christmas 91
Circumcision 22, 23, 79, 91
Commandment 24
Confessional 53
Confirmation 122
Constantine, Emperor 33, 62, 63, 115, 118
Constantinople 60, 63, 99
Copernicus 107
Corinth 62
Corpus Christi 92
Covenant 29, 87, 88, 92, 99, 109, 119
Creation 48, 126
Creed 60, 62, 63, 65, 106
Croagh Patrick, Ireland 129
Crucifixion 92
Crusades 128
Czestochowa, Poland 129

Darwin 37, 48
Deacons 114, 115
Decalogue 25, 39, 40, 48, 79, 80, 83, 95, 96
Deposit of Faith 106
Deuteronomy, Book of 23
Disciples 36
Dissolution of the Monasteries 26
Dogma 60, 103

Easter Sunday 92
Ecumenical Movement 28
Edessa 101
Egypt, Egyptian 18, 21, 31, 51, 58, 65, 86, 95
Elijah 89
Elisha 35
Epiphany 91
Eucharist 88, 89, 90, 92, 93, 98, 99, 103, 111, 121, 122
Exodus 49, 79, 92
Ezekiel 54, 55

Fatima, Portugal 129

Forgiveness 65, 66, 67, 68, 69, 122

Gabriel 94
Galileo 48, 49, 107
Gallienus, Emperor 33
Genesis, Book of 15, 35, 48, 49, 80, 86, 90, 126
Gentiles 98
Gilbert, W.S. 104
God's Forgiveness 50, 53, 54
God's Promise 21, 22, 29, 30, 53, 76, 77, 99, 119, 120, 122, 125, 126
Good Friday 92
Gospels 36
Grace 108, 109
Greece, Greek 10, 18, 25, 31, 79, 81, 97
Greek philosophy 25, 97
Guadalupe, Mexico 129

Hammurabi 39, 80
Hebrew 15, 17, 23, 25, 43, 47, 48, 49, 51, 60, 64, 65, 70, 74, 76, 77, 80, 81, 87, 88, 89, 91, 95, 96, 98, 107, 117, 118
Henry II 129
Henry VIII 28, 105, 106, 131
Heraclitus 10
Heresy 106
Herod 31
Hittite Code 80
Holy Orders 122
Holy Rosary 93
Holy Shroud of Turin 101, 102
Holy Spirit 62, 63
Holy Week 92

Iconoclasts 90, 98, 99
Icons 98, 99, 101
indefectability 104
Indulgences 107
Ireland 28
Isaac 15
Islam 25, 59, 98, 128

Israel, Israelite 21, 22, 58, 86, 110

Jacob 15
Jerusalem 13, 31, 86, 114, 117, 118, 128, 129, 131, 132
Jew, Jewish 22, 25, 26, 31, 32, 34, 39, 41, 79, 84, 89, 90, 95, 96, 97, 98, 102, 128
Jewish Sacred Scriptures 15
Job, Book of 81
John, John's Gospel 36, 98, 114, 124, 126
John the Baptist 36, 65
Jordan 47
Judaism 14, 15, 19, 22-25, 37, 39, 60, 77, 80, 94, 97, 98
Judges, Book of 65, 69

Karnak 18
Knock, Ireland 129

Last Supper 88, 92, 121
Law of God 39, 49, 50, 60, 80, 97
Lent 94
Leo X, Pope 105
Levi, Tribe of 110
Lourdes 129
Luke 36, 93, 98
Luther, Martin 28, 105

Maimonides 60
Mandylion 101
Mark, Mark's Gospel 36, 81
Marriage 122, 123
Mass 89, 90, 94, 103, 111, 126, 131
Matthew, Matthew's Gospel 36, 62, 69, 97, 114
Memphis 18
Mesopotamia 39, 79, 80
Messiah 31, 41, 44
Methodist 10
Monasteries 112
Monte Cassino, Italy 131
More, St Thomas 28

Mosaic Law 22, 23
Moses 65, 87, 95, 98
Muhammad 25, 43
Muslim 26, 59, 60, 128, 132
Mystery 50

Neighbour 59, 65, 80, 82, 95
Nero 32
New Learning 10
Nicaea, Council of 62, 63, 99
Nicene Creed 63
Nicodemus 103

Orange, Second Council of 109

Paganism 20, 21
Palestine 31
Palm Sunday 91
Passover 86, 88
Patriarchs 15, 17, 36, 77, 119
Patrick, St 129
Paul, The Apostle 50, 62, 92,
    98, 126
Penance 54
persecution 26, 28, 128
Persia, Persian 30
Peter, The Apostle 92, 103, 114,
    115, 129
Pharaoh 18
Plato 10
Pliny the Younger 33
Pontius Pilate 52, 114
Pope 103, 105, 115, 116
Pope John Paul II 9
Pope John XXIII 28, 29
Priesthood 116
Prophets 22, 30, 36, 37, 80,
    119, 126
Protestantism 41
Psalms, Psalmist 58

Reconciliation 68, 122
Reformation 41, 90, 106, 107,
    131
Renaissance 10, 28
Repentance 54

Resurrection 53, 89, 92, 94, 97,
    117, 126
Revelation 20, 62, 103
Rome, Roman 31, 32, 69, 70,
    81, 88, 92, 101, 103, 114,
    116, 118, 128, 129, 131, 132
Russell, Bertrand 11

Sacrament 121, 122
Sacrifice 14, 84, 85, 87, 88, 90,
    110
Samaritans 98
Scholastics 11
Second Vatican Council 28, 29
Septuagint 18
shrines 129
Simeon 91
sin 28, 39, 46ff
Spanish Inquisition 26
Suetonius 33
Sunday 91
Supreme Pontiff 129
Syria, Syrian 31

Tacitus 32
Temple at Jerusalem 86, 87, 88,
    89, 111, 114, 117, 129, 132
Ten Commandments, The 25,
    39, 40, 48, 79, 81, 98
Thales 10
Theodosius I, Emperor 63
Torah 23
Trajan 33
transubstantiation 90
Trent, Council of 90
Trinity 60, 61

Vatican/Council 49, 116
Virgin Mary 63, 92, 93, 103,
    118, 129

Walsingham shrine 129
Way of the Cross 94

Jahweh/Yahweh 23, 87, 127